ZEN IN ACTION

YOSH TAGUCHI, M.D.

ZEN IN ACTION

A surgeon reveals his life philosophy

Foreword by Howard M. Schwartz, B.A., M.Ed.

Guérin

© Guérin Publishers, 2006

4501, rue Drolet
Montréal (Québec)
H2T 2G2
Phone number: 514-842-3481
FAX: 514-842-4923
e-mail: francel@guerin-editeur.qc.ca
Web site: http://www.guerin-editeur.qc.ca

Legal deposit
ISBN-13: 978-2-7601-6943-2
ISBN-10: 2-7601-6942-X
Bibliothèque nationale du Québec, 2006
Bibliothèque et Archives Canada, 2006
Printed in Canada

We acknowledge the financial support of the Government of Canada through the Book Publishing Industry Development Program (BPIDP) for our publishing activities.

Canada

«Government of Quebec – Tax Credit Program on books edition – SODEC»

Société
de développement
des entreprises
culturelles
Québec

Sample cover Guérin, éditeur ltée
Photographs on the front cover Author's collection
Layout, computer graphics Guérin, éditeur ltée

Distribution

A.D.G.
4501, rue Drolet
Montréal (Québec)
H2T 2G2
Phone number: 514-842-3481
FAX: 514-842-4923

PHOTOCOPYING KILLS BOOKS

For the *issei*, like my mother and my late father, and for the *nisei*, like my older sister and younger brother, who bravely endured and, uncomplaining, made this land a better country.

Acknowledgement

It has become fashionable in recent years for people to record their family story as a document to treasure within the family. I may have started this book with such an intention but, along the way, became convinced that what I have learned over a lifetime could be of interest to those outside my immediate family.

I wish to thank Howard M. Schwartz for making my story flow in a more coherent manner. Items I had at the beginning of the account ended up towards the end and visa-versa. What I thought were minor points were expanded, while other areas were scaled down or eliminated. And the manuscript was improved.

I want to thank professor Joseph Hofbeck (and his wife, Genevieve), not only for rendering the book in French but for pointing out errors in the original English version and for making suggestions that I have adopted.

I need to thank Voyo Kovalsky for supplying me with many of the quotes that I have used. I wish to acknowledge roshi Victor Hori, Dr. Morel Bachinski, and the late professor Raymond Klibansky for providing me stimulating conversation that I have worked into the book. I want to thank Avi Morrow and Ashok Vijh for their friendship and encouragement. Finally, I want to thank my wife, Joan, my four children, Kathleen, Edwin. Jocelyn, Carolin, their partners, and the five grandchildren for their unconditional love and the continuing joy they bring into my life every day.

Table of contents

Foreword

I first met Yosh Taguchi about thirty years ago, when my G.P. said that "I should get that thing looked at by a specialist." I dutifully made the appointment, spent the requisite half-hour looking for a parking spot in the area, and ensconced myself in the large, rectangular waiting room of his office, not far from the Montreal Childrens' Hospital, on Tupper Street in the downtown Montreal area. I was surrounded by a group of about thirty worried men, all wondering what the good doctor would find, and all equally hoping that he would not have to use those evil catheters, which were stored on the shelf of the inner office. Even in those days, "Dr. Taguchi" was a known commodity, with a reputation for accurate diagnosis and treatment, so there was a small light at the end of the tunnel for us all, although it was small solace until we had been examined. Eventually my turn came, and when my name was announced by the businesslike nurse-receptionist behind the desk, I screwed up my courage and entered the examining room.

I was met by a smiling, affable man, who seemed to expend more energy merely asking pertinent questions, than I did playing tennis! To say that Yosh Taguchi was intriguing would be to say that a Ferrari was merely a car. He not only took my medical history, but I had the distinct impression that he was also taking the measure of my words, sorting and selecting, assigning weight and value, so that at the end of those few minutes he would have a picture of the man, as well as his symptoms. It was a feeling that would return in our later relationship together and would continuously remind me of the understated complexity of this remarkable surgeon. His advice to "Leave it alone and it will go away on its own," was accurate, and I returned to my normal way of life, happy that he had found nothing of interest.

Not too many years later, I read his first book "Private Parts," and took some pleasure in the fact that I had met the author himself.

Time has a way of catching up with us, however, and in the mid 1990's, I found myself looking for the good doctor once again. Arriving on the sixth floor of the Royal Victoria Hospital, I found myself surrounded by a sea of humanity; mostly male, and almost everybody waiting for the same man, who disappeared and reappeared with lightning speed, between the examining rooms further down the corridor. What was surprising, was the lack of concern about waiting to see 'him,' as he was called. No one needed to mention the name 'Yosh Taguchi' in this waiting area. The pronoun was good enough.

"Have you seen him before?" one would ask.

"He's been my doctor for twenty five years," another would say. Not to be outdone in the praise department, others would quietly chime in:

"He's terrific!"

"He operated on me two years ago and he saved my life **and** my marriage!"

"He listens and he gives you time!"

"Great guy!"

"Let me tell you, they don't come any better than this one!"

I felt reassured just to hear the praise coming from my fellow patients; not that their comments stilled my personal medical concerns, but they did reconfirm that I was in the right place.

When my turn came, I was surprised to see that he recalled my earlier visit. I mentioned that I had enjoyed reading his first book and he said that he 'just happened to have' the sequel "The Prostate," sitting on the shelf behind him. It wasn't long before I decided to give in to my curiosity and peruse the second in the series as well.

I told Dr. Taguchi that I was now retired, so that if he had another book in the works, I would be glad to do some editing for him. Little was I to know that this remark would lead to a collegial friendship and the birth of this third work. Not too long afterward, my telephone rang and, eighteen months, several reams of paper, five enjoyable working dinners and countless e-mails later, we "put this book to bed."

Before you read it, however, there are a few things you should know. Firstly, the two preceding books were medically-based, and therefore easier to write. They dealt with empirical fact, proven process and largely predictable results; hence, the flow of information was largely linear. In this autobiographical work, Yosh Taguchi has taken us on a 'stream of consciousness' trip, using theme and place as the anchors. He takes us on an intriguing journey, looking at every stop through the eyes, both of the younger "Yosh," and the now older "Dr. Taguchi." It is a voyage of self-revelation and no small amount of risk-taking, as he sets out both his beliefs and his biases. From the political to the religious; from the philosophical to new-age medicine, this book is more than an account of an individual's history. It is an intimate glimpse into the man himself.

With courage and determination, he pulls back the curtain of his youth in the internment camps, and allows us to see the effect of those years on a young Japanese boy. He brings us into his family, and gives us the privilege of meeting his parents. Above all, he takes us on an odyssey of belief and faith, culminating in his assertion that the "Zen" surgeon is the gold standard. It is a hard-hitting account of coming of age in a new country; a telling statement about the medical system, and a challenge to those who would be more complete as human beings.

For those of you who have had the honour of being treated by this physician, the book is a gift; a wonderful account of his life's work and beliefs. It helps to explain the degree of care and expertise he gives to each and every one of us, and in no small measure, explains his medical successes.

For the rest, who have not yet had the privilege of meeting Yosh Taguchi, this work is a text for life; a blueprint for thought; an appeal to reason, and a plea for understanding.

I can think of no finer legacy for such a worthy man.

Howard M. Schwartz B.A. M.Ed*
Montreal
November 2005

---

* Howard M. Schwartz is a retired educational administrator, who now consults in strategic planning and school success for school boards and administrators. He is also a professional speech-writer.

Introduction

No matter what the measuring stick or where the bar is set, and regardless of who is making the count or what the standard of reckoning, there can be no denying it – I have had a protracted education – twenty-six years of it. In fact, it took me an extra year, twelve years all together, to complete primary school and high school, four years to earn an undergraduate degree (B.Sc.), another four years to obtain a medical degree (M.D.), and finally, six more years to earn a Ph.D., and certification as a surgical specialist in Canada (FRCSC). I was living the adage: Education is my religion, knowledge my salvation. But, I must not forget an old proverb from Brazil – knowledge cuts up the world, wisdom makes it whole.

It is always pleasant to start a personal story with good news, so I chose the summer of 2001, and a crowded auditorium at McGill University in Montreal, where the Medical Faculty of my *alma mater* named me to the *Honours List for Educational Excellence*. It was a splendid and singular occasion – a culminating event in a long career, and a fulfillment of my cherished ambition to be recognized and appreciated as a surgeon-teacher by my peers. I placed it on the same level of importance as obtaining a government operating grant for medical research, getting a paper accepted for publication by a reputable journal, or having a manuscript accepted by a major publishing house – three events that I had deemed highlights of my career, until then.

I was the only surgeon on the list of seven doctors to be honoured that year. The other nominees were professors I admired from Anatomy, Oncology, Psychiatry, Nutrition and Food Sciences and Family Medicine. Dr. Yvonne Steinert, Associate Dean of Faculty Development, chaired the Awards Ceremony and she instructed me to come to the ceremony with a five-minute speech that had something to say about teaching.

I pondered a number of questions that came to my mind, and surprisingly few of them were directly related to teaching, although without exception, they all had much more to do with learning, culture and religion. Strangely enough, an awareness of my own cultural heritage was the dominating factor on my mind at that time. It was a fact of life that had permeated every aspect of my personal and professional existence until that day. Was my recognition "due to" or "in spite of" my Japanese-Canadian roots, I wondered, or did it in fact, count at all? The mind tends to wander at the strangest times, and I found myself thinking of a story I had heard as a child. I recalled to mind Momotaro, the peach pit boy of my childhood legends, in which a washerwoman and her husband find a large peach pit floating in a stream. When they break open the peach pit at home, a baby boy emerges. The peach pit boy (Momotaro) grows up to become an outstanding young man, who must eventually leave home in order to search out and slay the evil dragon. I never questioned how a boy could emerge from a peach pit, but my heart went out to the elderly couple who had worked so hard to raise a son, only to see him go off on a wild crusade. I wondered if I could compare my odyssey in medicine to such a life. I knew that my upbringing played a significant role in my eventual accomplishments, but that was only a part of the puzzle I now set myself; that of tracing my spiritual roots.

How much did I owe to my early Christian upbringing? Did the years of Sunday School and the interminable preaching really make a difference? What value did I assign to my embracing Zen in middle age? Was any part of my accomplishment due to a genetic endowment, and how much could I attribute to my tenacious pursuit of medicine as my goal?

In short, I pondered how much of life was, in fact, pure luck; how much, faith; how much, genetics; and how much just plain hard work?

I told Dr. Steinert that I was going to talk about "Zen and Surgery," and that is precisely what this book is all about.

The Nikkei *Connection*

As a toddler in Japan I was asked what I aspired to become when I grew up.

"I will be king," I replied.

"That is not possible!" the elders said, horrified at the arrogance of my response. (In a country where the people believe their king is descended directly from deity, it was an outrageous claim.) But, I did not persist as, perhaps, I should have.

"Why not?" I might have asked. Instead, I said:

"Then, I will become the person most important after the king!"

I have had a yo-yo relationship with my *nikkei* heritage – proud of it one moment, ashamed of it the next. The word, *"nikkei,"* I should explain, means being born of Japanese parents or at least to one parent with some degree of Japanese ancestry. I was Japanese at birth, the 25ᵗʰ of September, 1933, in a little hamlet called Honjyo. This small village is located in the district of Inae-mura, on the principal Japanese island of Honshu. I became Canadian by immigration; a despised and unwanted alien with the outbreak of World War II, and today, a bonafide, passionate, and patriotic citizen. On July 15th, 1937, before my fourth birthday, the ocean liner Hikawu-Maru, crossed the Pacific ocean from Yokohama to Vancouver, on a two week voyage that brought our family back to Canada. It was *back* because my parents and even my grandfather had lived in Canada before, and my older and only sister had been born in Vancouver.

I have only vague recollections of my life in Japan, but a few small events still stand out, as early childhood memories tend to do, even in later years. I recall being taken by motorcycle to watch a kite-flying event. The Japanese had elevated kite-making and kite-flying to new heights and I distinctly remember the brightly coloured structures in the shape of fish and dragons, soaring through the clear blue sky. I recall the feeling of wading in cold water just outside our house in order to lure fish into a trap. The fish were kept in man-made trenches until it was time to prepare one for dinner; a clever way to keep them fresh before the days of routine refrigeration. And I remember knocking my knees, repeatedly, on the rock hearth in our ancestral home. My roots, although planted in Japan, did not, unfortunately grow deep, and today I still feel estranged from that heritage.

I have no recollection at all of our arrival in Vancouver, except for a fleeting image of a pod of whales, breathing and spouting, as we passed by. I *do* know we somehow got to Port Hammond, a lumber town in the Fraser valley, where we would make our new home. The part of town in which we lived was virgin farmland, claimed from untamed forest by Japanese-Canadian farmers. Port Hammond has since changed its name to Maple Ridge and has become noteworthy for the athletes it has produced, among whom were the baseball player, Larry Walker, and the race car driver, the late Greg Moore.

My early childhood was filled with the sights and sounds of a typical mill town. At my neighbor's signal that dynamite set under a tree stump was about to be detonated, my small legs would run for the nearest cover, where I would wait in excited anticipation for the drama which would follow. A lot of yelling took place first, followed by a moment of total silence, and then there was a dull boom that made the earth shake. After the blast, I would rush to the site to examine the excavation created by the explosion. The tree stump lay always on its side, its tortuous roots forming intriguing, artistic shapes, like those in clouds or driftwood. Sometimes I could make out the form of an animal, or some mythical creature. All it would have taken was a little trimming to unmask the rough-sculptured form. The thunder of the explosion, the smoke and the artistry made this event a little boy's dream.

A short walk from the farmland where we lived took me into town, on the shores of the Fraser river, and to the saw-mill where my father worked, grading lumber. Further north, I could cross the railroad tracks where the heavy trains made their daily runs, shaking our house as they rumbled by. The tracks were forbidden grounds, but my friends and I, all Japanese-Canadians, would play near them, placing nails on them so that they would be flattened into flat, knife-like pieces by the steel wheels. We could not place coins on the track because we seldom had any; besides which, we were taught that the destruction of money was a sinful act. Sometimes, we would search the grounds between the tracks for "treasures" discarded from the moving train, not knowing that when the toilets were flushed they discarded waste into the ground below. Some treasures!

My mother had a group of close acquaintances, and this helped to add to my group of friends, as I accompanied her on some of her neighbourhood visits. I considered it a particular treat to join her on a visit to Sam's (Osamu) house, a few blocks away because Sam had the coolest collection of toys in the neighbourhood. They were kept in a big wooden box in a closet, and whenever we visited, Sam's mother would pull it out and dump the contents out onto the living room floor so that I could play with them while she chatted with my mother. Eventually, Sam's mother appeared with a steaming teapot and I would be treated to a cup of sea-weed tea (*kobu-cha*), a favorite beverage of mine to this day.

Sam was a few years older than we were. This made him the leader of the gang, and since he loved baseball, we were organized into an amateur league. Each of us had a favourite team, mine being the Detroit Tigers. You might think I chose them for their hitting or their pitching. Not so! I simply liked the fancy, embroidered "D" on their shirts; in fact I copied it and pinned the insignia to my t-shirt whenever we played. I never aspired to become a professional ball-player; my dream was to play one day for the "Asashi's", a Japanese-Canadian team that played against others in Vancouver.

My buddy Aki and of course, his aggravating kid brother, and Ronnie, the "king of the short hop" added to this collection of friends. Summers passed into autumns, with the happy cries of "Safe!" and 'Out!' to be arbitrated by volume, if not by skill. Sam became an ordained protestant minister and Aki's snotty kid brother, a PhD marine biologist of some repute. I don't know what happened to Ronnie.

In short, between playing tag, hide and seek, and "kick the can," I was truly no different from any other young boy, except for the fact that I was unknowingly and unwillingly, to be marked forever by the second world war.

War Camps

December 7th, 1941 became memorialized as the "day of infamy" as US president, Franklin Delano Roosevelt labeled it. For Canadians of Japanese ancestry, this date was the end of our age of innocence. Before the war, the Japanese immigrants on the west coast of Canada had been successful fishermen and begrudgingly respected farmers. The fishermen were part of a thriving coastal industry, while the farmers were instrumental in converting a tangled forest into fertile farmland, *but* their untiring work habits, combined with the difference in their skin color, made them ready targets for racial discrimination. The surprise attack on Pearl Harbor simply rationalized the smoldering racism. As in the USA, Canadians of Japanese ancestry were rounded up for placement into camps created in the interior of British Columbia, far from the coast, away from potential sabotage.

Not all Canadians approved this relocation, this uprooting of innocent families. The military brass was against it, cognizant of the fact that

Canadians of Japanese origin had served honour-
ably during the first World War. Certain legislators
and many clergymen were also against such
blatant discrimination, but their voices were
drowned out by less tolerant neighbors, as
politicians seized the opportunity to advance their
own agendas.

I lived through that trying time as a child, and
I remain confused to this day about many events
that transpired, both physically and emotionally. I
was simply too young to fully comprehend what
was happening. Emotions within the Japanese-
Canadian community were running sky high.
Normally quiet unobtrusive people assaulted my
young ears with their high-pitched and strident
voices. Public gatherings became forums for
concern and even fear. Government decrees
announced: "No lights after sundown!" Rumors
suggested that Japanese-Canadian homes were
being targeted for vandalism under the protection
of darkness. The turmoil was unrelenting. Each day
brought more bad news. Facts were unclear. Truth
was distorted. And, of course, parents tried, albeit
in vain, to shield the children from the ugliness that
was pervasive.

I have vivid memories of the older Japanese-
Canadian students telling me that our school
principal had announced "When the Jap bombs rain
down on the school, the white children are to take
refuge in the basement while the Jap children are
to remain in their seats in the classrooms." Whether
or not they were telling the truth is not the critical

issue. It is the fact that I still remember the words today, which makes this chapter in my eight-year-old life, so significant.

I remember that in the midst of this terrifying time, all able-bodied men were rounded up to help construct the "relocation" camps that had to house 22,000 Japanese-Canadians identified as living on the west coast, thus working covertly, it was presumed, for the Japanese military regime. My father was sent away. This left our home and ourselves defenseless – and it left me fatherless, confused, and angry.

In the Spring of 1942, fearful of lynch mobs, as we had no adult male protection, a neighbor devised a simple alarm. Small pebbles were placed in tin cans, which were joined with cords, strung from one house to the other. To sound the alarm, jerking the string would cause the pebbles to rattle in the neighbor's house. Thankfully, the alarms were never sounded., but the sight of the can in our home, was a constant reminder that we were living in a hostile and frightening place. In early summer we were given two weeks' notice to reduce our belongings to twenty five pounds per child and one hundred pounds per adult. Anything in excess of these weights could be stored with a government appointed "custodian" or sold for a pittance. We were to be sent to a holding center in Hasting's Park, part of the Pacific Exhibition grounds, until the camps were ready to receive us.

The horses and cows were moved out and we were moved in. The stench of the animals still pervaded the premises; another reminder of our place on the social scale in those days. Double decker bunk beds with straw mattresses were set up in rows, and that collection of smelly furnishings became our domicile. The only privacy we had was provided by blankets, stretched around the bed posts, and because all the blankets were a uniform army grey, it was easy to get lost. In fact, I did a few times; a frightened eight-year-old, searching in a sea of same-grey blankets, for his mother. We lined up to be fed at a communal mess hall and we shared toilet and washing facilities with countless others. Hasting's Park was, for me, the worst experience of the war years. I couldn't stomach the food. The smell of manure killed my appetite as I lined up for the meals. I played with my meal to fool my mother but I couldn't swallow it. Sweet corn was bland and tasteless; nor did it help to overhear that the corn we ate was actually meant to feed hogs. There was so much flour added to the omelette that it looked and tasted like a spoiled cake. People milled about aimlessly, loudspeakers blared orders, and everybody looked frightened. I wet the bed. I wondered how long our confinement in this veritable prison was going to last, and how was I going to survive it. What was most frightening, however, was not knowing what the future held. We were there for only two weeks, but to my young mind, it was an eternity.

From Hasting's Park, our next destination was an abandoned ghost town, sixteen miles from a place ironically called, Hope, B.C. The relocation camp was given the name Tashme, after Taylor, Shirra, and Mead, three men responsible in some way for its construction. The camp accommodated more than two thousand people, the vast majority of whom were housed in three-room tar-papered shanties. Each hut had two bedrooms and a common kitchen. Water was brought in from wells outside, and one outhouse served several huts. Heat to cook the meals, was provided by a wood-burning stove while a kerosene lamp provided light. This ramshackle arrangement was considered sufficient to house two full families, and that's the way it was for most of our friends and neighbours.

My father chose to settle our family in one room of a large two-storied barn which was known as the "apartment." The two floors of the barn were divided into a series of rooms with a central hallway. At one end there was a common kitchen with a number of wood-burning stoves, each one to be shared by two families. Half-way down the hall, there were two toilets, but there were no sinks. Toilet tissue was a rare commodity, and the thick Eaton's catalogue often served as a functional substitute. Pages were torn out, folded, and softened by rubbing them together in the same way handkerchiefs are hand-washed. The accommodation in the "apartment" was more cramped, I think, than that in the huts. Each room could accommodate two double-decker bunk beds, a table with benches, place for a trunk or two, and some "walk-around space." The apartment, however, had electric lighting (although the fuse was set to blow whenever something more than a light bulb was plugged in), and it had flush toilets.

My father cut a hole in the ceiling, which gave us access to the attic of our second floor room. He then built a ladder, hinged on top, so that it could be pulled up by ropes to lie flat against the ceiling. When the ladder was lowered, it provided entry to a second room or, at least, to a storage room, built above the ceiling.

Although a number of families proposed sharing a shanty with us, my parents rejected the offers. They felt we would be better off with more privacy in the one room. Privacy was a rare commodity though, often more apparent than real. Youngsters living in the apartment or in the hut overheard things not really meant for children's ears. Whether that was good or bad is a debatable point, but I think it forced us to grow up sooner than anyone would have preferred. Decisions which might have a profound impact on the community, were discussed in committee by the elders of our group. I remember a gathering of adults in our one room, late one night, when the adults believed I was fast asleep. I heard my parents debating whether they should sanction the coupling of a man and a woman. The woman was a young widow; the man separated from his wife and family, still in Japan. "Why not a marriage of sorts?" it was argued, as the future was so uncertain. I remember thinking: What was there to argue? A man and a woman together should cope

better than either one alone. At the time I was
unaware of the implications of "coupling."

I don't know why the other families chose the
apartment over the shanties but, the children of
this dwelling turned out remarkably well. It is
quite astonishing that the fifteen or so "apartment"
families who remained in Canada after the war,
gave rise to no less than twenty-five children. From
that number, three boys became doctors, three
became dentists, four became engineers, one an
architect, and another a biochemistry professor
and that is, in all likelihood, an incomplete count.
At least three girls became university graduates,
two with doctorates, in the Sciences. Many of these
individuals remain my friends to this day.

Thankfully, life in the relocation camps bore
no comparison to the Nazi camps in Europe during
the same period. At the same time, any adult male
who had the gumption to protest loudly or
vigorously was placed in a separate barbed-wire
enclosed "prisoner-of-war" camp located outside the
province. He had to a wear prison garb with a red
circle emblazoned on its back while armed men
from the military watched over him. As far as I
know, not one prisoner tried to escape. Recently, I
met a retired military man who had served as a
prison guard at Angler, in northen Ontario, and he
asked if I could introduce him to anyone who might
have been his prisoner. I broached the subject with
men whom I knew had spent the war years as
prisoners-of-war, but not one of them wanted to
relive that part of his life, even in conversation.

For the younger children, like myself, however, the experience was a bit like going on a protracted camping trip with limited provisions, as people enjoy doing today. That is, in fact, how most of my friends and I remember the days in the camps. We choose to forget the indignities and remember the more enjoyable moments. Older children and adults whose lives were more seriously affected, recall the experience differently. In fact, many of them will not permit the subject to be broached. It is just too painful.

As a Physician, it amazes me today that more than two thousand people — men, women, and children, could have been placed in such primitive quarters for four long years without an outbreak of cholera or some other infectious disease occurring. In fact, there were no epidemics of any kind in any of the camps that housed so many segments of the uprooted twenty-two thousand people. The outhouses in Tashme, as in other camps, were treated regularly with caustic lime, and there was no contamination of the drinking water. Perhaps the sub-arctic temperature helped because the only sickness of consequence was tuberculosis, which necessitated the occasional patient being sent away to a TB sanitarium. In fact, my first teacher in the make-shift school had to be sent away because she had contracted this disease.

Although we were virtual prisoners during those years, we strove to maintain a semblance of normalcy in the camps. The will to be free is stubborn and strong. We could not liberate our bodies, but our minds and souls were an altogether different story. The evenings were filled with the sights and sounds of talent shows, amateur theater, and a showing of Japanese movies at regular intervals. Robert (Bobby) Ito, who has since had a successful career in Hollywood, was a regular performer. His rendition of the "*White Cliffs of Dover*" was eagerly anticipated at every concert. It is curious that such an anglophile song should have been so popular, but that is exactly how ambivalent the community was at the time. On one occasion a cake baked at the apartment was topped with an icing in the form of the naval flag of Japan – a rising sun with radiating red spokes. Everybody admired it. Then, one lady created a commotion by asking who was going to desecrate the flag by cutting into it.

Japanese language plays, known as "shibai" encouraged us to retain the feeling of cultural unity. These were the products of local talents, who wrote the scripts, designed the costumes, and constructed the sets, props and lighting. These productions had all the elements of the formal Kabuki theater, and also, understandably, the polish of an amateur high school production. Nevertheless, a few men and women gained notoriety and made repeat appearances, to the great delight of their growing fans.

A Mr. Tsuyuki was the projectionist for the Japanese movies. He sat alone in a cubicle which was hung from the ceiling, and he provided all the voices and the sound effects. This versatile vocalist had me fooled into believing that Japanese actresses were picked for their husky voices. After the samurai movies we would play at being samurai, fashioning swords from sticks in the same manner as other children played at being cops and robbers. One particular samurai movie made a lasting impression. It opens with a bandit whispering to the samurai hero in front: "Don't look back.... (ushiro wo miruna)" as he grimaces menacingly, sword held high. The sharp blade of the "katana" glistens in the evening light. The samurai walks confidently ahead, seemingly unfazed and unafraid. Suddenly the hero turns around, sword drawn, and in short order, cuts down the assailant with a single stroke. Then he wipes clean the blood stained blade of his samurai sword and returns it to the scabbard at his side. Somewhere near the end of the film, he is prostrate, mortally wounded, and he writes a message with his finger using his own blood as the ink.

I could never decipher what he had written, but I was always impressed with its dramatic impact, no matter how many times I saw the same movie. It was a link to the past and it also kept me from thinking too much about my reality at bedtime.

Every week, we lined up for our ration of one chocolate bar per person. Firm bars, like "O Henry" or solid chocolate, like Neilson's Nut Chocolate were the most popular because they lasted longer. Late-comers got the soft marshmallow-covered cakes. Radio was contraband but a few were smuggled in, and the progress of the war was transcribed onto mimeographed paper and circulated around the camp. Although the adults took some solace at being kept up-to-date, the children were not helped in any way by the news, and our confusion grew as the war went on.

Lighter Moments

I was too young to join the scouts, but old enough to be accepted into the Wolf Cub pack with friends of my age. This called for the purchase of a cap, sweater, and a kerchief and although our family did not have much money to spare in those days I did not feel guilty about that expense. I devoted myself diligently to these activities, and sported my allotment of the precious skill badges, which were awarded for proficiency in everything from signal flags to tying knots, a handy skill for a surgeon-to-be.

I am in the middle row, 7th from the left end, above the "cub".

/ST TASHME WOLF CUB PACK.
AUGUST 26TH, 1944.

Then came the announcement that judo lessons were to be introduced in camp. I begged my mother to make me a judo outfit, so that I could participate. The outfit could have been purchased, but I did not want to force that expense on my parents, so when she presented me with a complete uniform, made from the equivalent of potato sacks, I proudly accepted it. Eventually, we all participated in a tournament which attracted a huge audience. I was totally preoccupied with how I would perform, and petrified at being embarrassed in front of my parents and my peers. When it became my turn to engage in combat, I made the customary bow and approached my opponent with as much confidence as I could muster. He grabbed the lapel of my outfit and casually tossed me before I knew what was happening. That was one of several moments in my young life that I wish I could live again. The feel of the mat on my back was a far reaching second to the wound inflicted on my pride that day. Nevertheless, I was one of three cubs singled out for commendation by the wolf cub master and I received a set of camping dishes and an impressive certificate, which I have in my possession to this day. I don't know what I did to impress the people who made the choices, but I suspect it was my enthusiasm.

My experience as an honourary Detroit Tiger, coupled with Sam's coaching, convinced me that I was an expert baseball player so, brimming with the confidence of youth, I started my own league.

I soon found out that superstars must be able to hit the ball past second base, and I relegated myself to defense, where I made an adequate niche for myself and my home-made equipment. My basketball career took the same turn until someone told me that you could take a step or two with the ball before shooting. That fact, coupled with the reality that I was never going to be six feet tall, mandated my place on the team.

As far as the more expensive sports were concerned, I missed the two-wheeler my father had given me just before the evacuation, but otherwise I felt no sense of deprivation. The circumstances only made us all more creative. I recall tying a thread to the leg of a bumble-bee and flying it like a kite. I also learned how to catch a house fly with my bare hand. The trick was to pass an open hand quickly over a fly that had perched and then to close the hand loosely with the fly inside. Then, by throwing the fly hard against a floor, it could be killed outright or stunned enough to be dealt with. My children have watched me do this decades later inside our house. It is only a small feat, I know; however, it counted me among the mighty and talented where my younger children were concerned. Glory can be found in the most unlikely places when you are "Dad."

One activity I abhorred in Tashme was the after-school Japanese lessons. My teacher was a strict disciplinarian and those of us who were less conscientious about our homework were always being singled out for repeated reprimand and ridicule. The do-gooders were always being praised, but damned if I was ever going to be caught among the sycophants. Today I regret that I spent more energy trying to evade the work than in trying to learn. I have only a rudimentary knowledge of the Japanese language as a consequence, and a rich part of my heritage has disappeared as a result.

War

I remember being confused about my allegiance to Canada. I was rebelling, both consciously and sub-consciously, because of the mixed messages I was receiving at every turn. There was a tension between the *Nikkei* "Yoshinori" and the Canadian "Yosh" and the loyalties expected of each. Was it not the very people who disrupted my life who were now intent upon imposing "school", and was it not my duty to defy such an imposition? Why was I being told to be a good Canadian? If I was *Nikkei*, weren't they the enemy? Even the schoolbooks we received, were modified so as to reflect western values and culture. The page in the Japanese language primer that said: "Forward, forward, soldier go forward" (Susume, susume, haitai susume) was pasted shut, while we were taught to sing: "Onward, Christian soldiers, marching as to war." Despite the fact that we were virtual prisoners in our own country, we were encouraged to collect rubber bands and silver foil from the cigarette packages to help the war effort. Even these cardboard wrappers were a constant reminder that we were at war, as the cigarette manufacturers had emblazoned the covers with pictures of warplanes, both allied and axis.

At one time the camp received a shipment of Japanese goods – authentic Kikkoman soy sauce, bean paste (miso) and other food-stuffs from the government of Japan, courtesy of the Red Cross. Did that mean that Japan was aware of our plight and cared for us? The gift from Japan was particularly puzzling to me. Did it not make more sense to be a loyal Japanese? My parents seemed set on being good Canadian citizens, but my mind occupied a no-man's land with reference to the words "loyalty" and "patriotism."

I had, by that time, been cajoled into believing that our survival depended upon being good Canadian citizens. That was the way to persuade the Canadian government it had made a mistake in consigning us to the camps – and the way to eventual vindication. To a young Japanese-Canadian with a developing sense of allegiance, a Nikkei heritage, and no trustworthy elders upon whom to rely for guidance, these days were confusing and troubling.

Childhood Memories

My brother was born in November, 1943. He was the first child born of parents in the "apartment," and he was lovingly cared for by all our neighbors on the floor. At the time of my brother's birth, the camp dentist's wife also gave birth to a son. My mother claims that the dentist's baby cried incessantly because his mother could not produce enough milk; and so my mother, being the selfless person she was, served as his wet nurse. The dentist's son grew up to become a prominent architect in Vancouver, my brother became a surgeon, a professor at Queen's university in Kingston, Ontario and I became a urologist with a McGill staff appointment.

The lure of medicine started for me in the internment camp, partly, because I loved the aroma of phenol that permeated the first-aid station where my father worked. He was a licenced masseur and was thus appointed to a position in health-care. Because of his training, he became the first-aid technician for the men who worked the saw-mill or gathered the lumber. I was a frequent visitor to the clinic and I was impressed with the high regard the men had for the first-aid man, my father! They would come with cuts and bruises, and he would bandage their wounds, give them pills, and offer them stern instructions about what to do and, more importantly, about what *not* to do. Many of these lumberjacks were robust men, much bigger and muscular than he was, but they listened to his instructions respectfully, accepting him almost as a father-figure. They never once challenged his advice. I was impressed with that. As well, the dentist who worked with my father, rewarded me with the empty vials of the local anaesthetic he used. The glass vial was corked at each end with a rubber plug. When I pushed one plug towards the other with a chop-stick, I could convert the empty vial into a pop gun. Needless to say, I practiced my marksmanship on any wayward fly, ant, or spider in the vicinity, most often missing by a good margin. I also used the vials to store the juices of different plants, leaves, and insects. I discovered that many juices were bitter and, fortunately, I was unaware that the leaves of certain plants could be poisonous. Some juices changed the colour of flames, some made them sparkle, and some had no effect at all. I thought however, that I was discovering secrets unknown to mankind. This era of my life awakened in me a curiosity as to how things worked, a trait which I bring to my research to this very day, but the truth of the matter is that I survived that phase of my life more by good luck than by good judgement.

After three years in Tashme, our family was moved to New Denver, a deserted mining town in the Kootenays. Unlike Tashme, which was cold and inhospitable, New Denver was a veritable geo-graphical paradise. The town was built on the shores of Slocan lake and was not totally isolated. There were a handful of local white residents, actually Doukhobors, from Russia. They were quiet, decent people, who made their living from orchards of apple, pear and cherry trees. The fruit trees were not fenced in, and we treated ourselves to the ripe harvest on a regular basis. The Doukhobors, bless their generous hearts, made little fuss of our theft. Rumor of the fact that they danced naked around bonfires were overrated, as I never once saw this taking place.

I remember the year in New Denver as one filled with fun; in the water skinny-dipping off the wharf, on the mountain slopes on home-made skis, and particularly, in the communal bath houses.

These were constructed in the Japanese fashion. A large rectangular wooden vat which could seat twenty people along a bench on its inner rim, was filled with water, which flowed in through a trough from the outside. A serrated wooden platform rested on a copper bottom, below which a fire was lit. When the water got too hot, more water would be let in. A large area outside the tub was meant for washing and the tub was supposed to be used only for soaking. Many children learned to swim in the tub, starting with the dead man's float and progressing to the dog paddle. There were bath-houses for men and adjoining ones for women; thus the sexes were separated but the age groups were not. Dirty old men, pedophiles, in fact, were constantly trying to grab us. They never succeeded because we were too quick and nimble for them. Only in later years did I understand that we were indiscriminately thrown into a bathhouse in the company of the very few sexually deviant denizens of our community, a surprising occurrence, considering the high moral values which existed in the camps.

An interest and curiosity about the opposite sex was emerging among us and we often tried to sneak a peek into the female bathhouse, separated from the male side by a thin wooden wall. Once, a knot in the wood plank came loose and fell out. We could place our eyes against the hole and see the other side. All we saw, unfortunately for us, were amorphous bodies hidden behind a fog of steam.

The wharf in New Denver was located adjacent to the bath house. This gave us the opportunity to skinny-dip, and when sufficiently chilled, head to the bath house for a warm soak. One thing we did still gives me the shivers. Challenging ourselves as to who was the bravest, we would jump off one side of the wharf, and with our breath held, make our way under water to the other side.

I suspect that there was a guardian angel who protected us from our own follies in those days. Slocan lake was two miles wide; in fact, from one side of the lake one could readily see the other on a clear day. As we had no canoes or row-boats to play with, we made rafts by nailing logs together. With these, we ventured onto the water, hoping there would be no gust of wind to take us out beyond the point of safe return.

While the lake provided us with a recreational setting in the summer months, it was the mountains which were the arena for us in the wintertime. Home-made skis were constructed from fresh hardwood planks. The front end was fashioned into a point, then turned up under steam, and held in that position with a rope and nail until it dried. The bottom was planed and sanded to a smooth surface. An inner-tube from a bicycle wheel made the straps. Candle wax was applied to help the glide, but there was no central groove nor sharp edge to help to establish control. In our previous home in Tashme nobody had skied, as the valley had been too flat and the distant mountains, outside our area of confinement. Not so in New Denver! We hurtled down the mountain side, flailing at the white slopes with sticks as ski poles, arriving at the bottom of the hill winded and exhilarated. In New Denver I saw the occasional adult with real ski equipment, but people on real skis negotiated the slopes no better than we did. In my youthful exuberance, I surmised that our home-made skis were better.

Other children slid down little hills in home-made sleds and found that cardboard worked better than anything manufactured. It was a tribute to the ingenuity and craftsmanship of our parents that we were able to enjoy the winters as we did.

When I think about it now, my parents did not intrude upon my freedom to play as I wished. Perhaps they trusted my survival instinct or, perhaps, they were preoccupied with my younger brother who was now two years old and given to wandering off on a regular basis. I would not have been upset had life in New Denver lasted longer. I knew, though, that this camp was our home for a limited time, and this feeling was confirmed, as the war ended not long after our arrival. Our family was shunted out of Tashme because that camp was designated as a relocation site for those who wished to be repatriated to Japan. It is interesting to note that the word "repatriated" was used even then, to apply to loyal Canadians. I know my parents took some heat for not signing the document to return us all to Japan. They had, after all, a house to which they could go. My father and mother were simply convinced that life for the children would be better in Canada than in a land that had just lost a war. I felt they were making significant sacrifices on our behalf, and I therefore committed myself to succeed in my studies. We were detained in New Denver until the summer of 1946, when we were advised we could relocate anywhere in Canada, except British Columbia, where we were still not welcome. This ban was finally lifted in 1949.

My parents consulted my sister about the decision to stay in Canada, but I was not a part of that process. I'm not sure which way I would have voted if I had been given the choice. More likely than not, I would have opted for Japan. I felt I was a second class citizen in this country and I was still having problems with my l's and r's; a small pronunciation problem if you are "one of the boys" but a significant hurdle to overcome if you are *Nikkei*.

Heading East

My father and mother chose Montreal as our desired destination. It was rumored that there was less racism in French-Canada, that jobs were available, and that my mother could find work because she could sew. My sister was delighted. She knew that Montreal was the home of a world-class university called McGill.

Despite the fact that we were technically "free," we were to be sent to another holding center located in Farnham, in the Eastern Townships, fifty miles from Montreal. It was then being used as a camp for captured German officers. The officers were moved out and we were moved in. There was no question that this was quite an upgrade from the animal quarters of Hasting's Park and the huge barn we called the apartment. The house we occupied had hardwood floors and fancy light fixtures on its walls. We had to walk a mile for our meals, though.

My sister left shortly afterwards to work as a live in baby-sitter for a family in Outremont, a well-to-do suburb within the city of Montreal, while she got ready to enroll in a local high school. The rest of us spent the summer adjusting to life outside the war camps of British Columbia.

Two events still stand out in my memories of Farnham. The first was treasure hunting with my newly made Japanese-Canadian friends at a nearby giant junk-yard. The place may have been fenced off, but the metal pile of junked old cars was too enticing an attraction. I remember sitting behind the steering wheel of an old Chevrolet, and driving it on great journeys in my mind. The junkyard was also a treasure trove of ball-bearings, springs and even an old compass, all of which were carted home and lovingly hidden under our beds. Thinking about it now, it was a dangerous place to play, as jagged metal on this precarious pile could have come tumbling down at any time. It was not long after we were seen there a few times that the expected announcement was made in the cafeteria.

"Some boys were seen at the junk-yard. The place is off-limits and I do not intend to repeat this warning," the commandant said.

"I wonder who those boys were?" my mother said.

"Hmmm," I replied

This was typical of my relationship with my mother, who was never direct with her criticism or reprimands. She relied on the unspoken word and the implied suggestion. Evoking shame was a tactic she found very effective in the raising of her three children. The technique must have worked, as I find myself mirroring her from time-to-time with my own.

The joy of fishing for rock bass in very shallow running water, among big boulders has to take second place among my Farnham "gems". The fish were no more than five inches long, but they had long jagged spikes in their dorsal fins. It was not easy removing the fish from the hook without getting nicked by the spikes, but the reward was worth the effort. This was totally different from the trout fishing I had been used to. In Tashme, there were many brooks nearby, just like the ones I had fished in before the war, but fish hooks were a rare and precious commodity. I tried to make one from a safety pin but, without the barb, it was an exercise in futility. The few hooks I possessed had to be used with extraordinary care. One time I resorted to fishing where the creek had formed a clear basin. I could lie on a fallen tree, look down and search for a brown stick that would turn to silver when the trout lurched forward. I lowered my line and waited for the trout to see the worm wriggling on the hook. The trout, however, was not interested in the worm. It approached the deadly hook, sniffed, and swam away. In frustration, I cast the line, got snagged, and lost my precious hook. I learned then and there that an act carried out in frustration can be detrimental. As physicians, we should be mindful of this possibility, as the resulting problems can be irreparable.

I did have some success at fishing, however, and so the reader should not think me totally inept at this sport, let me tell you the one about the important fish that did not get away.

I caught my first trout, before the war, in a brook in Port Hammond. I couldn't believe my luck. I placed the fish in a brown paper bag and tucked it inside my shirt for safe-keeping. The trout, perhaps six inches long, was still alive and wiggled inside the paper bag making loud noises as it flapped against the paper. It stopped for a moment, and wriggled again. Then, as I held my breath, the trout stopped wriggling, and when I breathed in, it came back to life. I could control the life of my trout, or so I thought! Eventually, though, the flapping stopped no matter what I did with my breath. I wondered then, and sometimes now, as to what we can do when we wish to prolong life. Can we will a fellow creature to do so? What *do* we wish for as physicians when human life approaches its inevitable end? I wonder ... are we the fishermen, or just a larger trout in the scheme of things?

Montreal

In the fall of 1946, our family settled in Montreal. We arrived at Windsor Station on a Canadian Pacific Railway train. My first memorable sight was the line of caleches just outside the station. The four- wheeled carriages were brightly painted and drawn by a huge horses of varying colours, ranging from chestnut, to pure black. Some wore ear-muffs and others had decorative studs on their leather strapping, but they all had thick, workmanlike legs. These horse drawn carriages competed with the automobiles for the rights to the downtown streets. With a resounding "clippety-clop," they sauntered down the cobblestones, pausing now and then to relieve themselves, oblivious to the passers-by. The horse drawn carriages were also used to deliver milk and bread, I soon discovered. Borden's milk and Wonder bread, I remember, came to us that way. My favourite vehicles, however, were the trucks that were modified to prepare and sell French fries on the streets of the city. I would soon learn that they serviced the schools, coming around at recess and lunch time. The hot fries were sold in small brown paper bags, seasoned with salt and vinegar, and they were delicious. I was envious of friends who had regular pocket money to spend. The only time I was certain to have loose change in my pocket was when I went to Sunday School, and the money was for the collection.

Trudging up the winding outside staircases, men hauled blocks of ice on their shoulders, to feed the ice-boxes in the east end of the city where we lived. The brick, stone, and concrete buildings were overwhelming, as was the cacophony of city sounds — the screech of streetcars, the blare of car horns and the deafening sirens of ambulances and fire trucks. Pretty ladies with bright red lips and golden hair, men in suits and ties, and nuns in their habits, rounded out this panoply of sights and sounds. In the preceding four years I had not seen automobiles, paved streets, street-cars, brick houses or people in fancy clothes. My little brother, now three, was actually terrified. He came running home because he had seen a pair of legless women in black, dressed up to look like penguins.

On my first excursion on a streetcar, I was given a quarter to purchase a booklet of tickets. I deposited the quarter into the ticket box and there was a major commotion before my "generosity" was rectified. Had I been told the quarter would buy an entire package of tickets, it could have saved us all a lot of embarrassment. It was only one example of the many elementary things I had to learn. I was like a stroke victim, having to relearn how to walk and talk except, for me, it was for the first time. I was taken by a family friend to Montreal's Botanical Garden, situated on a street called Pie IX, which was strangely pronounced 'pee noof'. I found out that a bicycle had to be negotiated with caution on streetcar lines as its wheels were just the right size to be trapped in the grooves of the tracks. I also learned which streets were safe and which were not. City streets may have been public property, but were treated as private by the street gangs. There was an undeclared war between the French speaking boys and the English speaking boys, like the battle between the whites and Latinos in New York city.

Strangers, young and old, stared at me, and the young brazen ones called me "Chink." or "Jap." From time to time a gang of youths would try to engage me in a fight. They would surround me and shove forward a youngster slightly smaller than me. He would taunt me expecting me to launch an attack. I knew that if I hit someone smaller than myself it would provide an excuse for the bigger boys to pounce on me, so I swallowed my pride and walked away. Once though, I challenged a bigger boy to a one-on-one fight, but warned him that I was trained in judo. I must admit, I was secretly relieved when he declined.

I also acquired a paper route. Shortly after our arrival, I saw some boys at a bus stop near our house. They collected a wagon full of newspapers, French and English, and prepared them for home delivery. I asked the grumpy old man in charge if he was looking for more help, and I was hired on the spot. My sack of papers was heavy, as I had twice the pile of the other boys, but I quickly learned the route and got used to the routine of delivering papers after school every day. On weekends I had to make the rounds again for the weekly collection. This was more difficult, as many people did not answer the doorbell, although I knew they were in. Interestingly, the collections that were the most difficult were often from better homes. I learned that the most considerate people were not always the most well-off. People in the most modest homes, I discovered, often tipped me the most. This was an observation I later had confirmed when I joined the burgeoning hotel industry in the lower Laurentian Mountains, not far north of Montreal.

Becoming Canadian

As an adolescent, I was ashamed of my Japanese roots. The pervasive western propaganda had become a part of me, and I could not think of the Japanese as other than psychopathic people, capable of the most heinous crimes without the slightest sense of guilt. I truly believed that they were uncaring of all lives including their own, as long as they could shout "banzai" with their final breaths. Furthermore, I did not like my Japanese appearance. My straight black hair was too thick and too unmanageable, my short sightedness necessitated thick, clumsy glasses, and my diminutive stature made me feel like a dwarf. I yearned to be tall, and white, with wavy blonde hair. Indeed, I was like a banana; yellow on the outside, white on the inside, sweet and mushy, and possessing no backbone.

The emergence of pride in my Japanese ancestry coincided with the re-emergence of Japan as a nation, rising like a phoenix from its atomic ashes after World War II. In all probability, any potential pride in my Japanese ancestry might have remained crushed, repressed forever, if Japan had not resurrected itself; but, slowly and surely, Japanese goods were becoming identified as being of fine quality and high standards. The fact that this excellence pervaded all its consumer goods, from cameras to automobiles, and only served to reinforce my slowly-emerging sense of identity. The Japanese had adopted the doctrines of the American, W. Edwards Deming: "Make one product, make it well, then move on to the next."

The Japanese before the war had been intransigent and militant. After the war they became docile and obedient, at least to the world's face. Their ability to adapt to changing circumstances served them well. It is a racial characteristic that may well be genetic, although I would be hard-pressed to provide empirical evidence of this theory.

As Japan blossomed as an economic power, I grew in stature, too. I could follow an oversized Anglo-Saxon predecessor to a podium, lower the microphone amid giggles and say: "Long ago, I discovered that height was not everything in life!" to appreciative applause. Like sushi and sashimi, I was in demand, attractive even to good-looking members of the opposite sex. I discarded my hyphenated status. I was no longer a Japanese-Canadian. I had finally become Canadian.

I have a Japanese first name, "Yoshinori", unlike my older sister and younger brother, who, having been born in Canada, have both English and Japanese first names. Even my father, whose name is Zenichi, had a western first name, "Edwin", assigned to him by a teacher when he started school in Canada. I seldom use my official full name, preferring to use the first four letters, "Y-o-s-h". This is pronounced like "wash" or "gosh". I like the name; however, it is not Japanese, as there is no such word in the Japanese lexicon. The Japanese would have shortened it to a Yo, Yoshi, or Yoshio. Yosh is a name like "Sony." The giant Japanese corporation adopted this name after much deliberation because they liked the sound and look of it and felt it would be well accepted around the world. I'd like to think I did the same thing with my name, although many years ahead of Sony.

Yosh will do for my new Canadian status, but I was less prepared to be reminded that I was not really Japanese on one of my visits to my ancestral home; far from it! My own relatives put me in a taxicab in Japan and told the driver to: "Take this gaijin (foreigner) to the Okura hotel." How fortunate for me that I had already completed the intellectual and emotional transition, with reference to my identity, or these words might have stung with much greater force than they did.

Travels to the Orient - Japan

My father with his cousin who spruced up our ancestral home, with me holding a picture of our family emblem

I have made four trips to Japan since my parents brought me away from the island, just before my fourth birthday in 1937. The first return trip occurred in 1982. Its purpose was to bring the branches of our family together; however, it taught me something of the complexities of Japanese life and customs – an enigma for me even today. Before our family reunion, my father's well-to-do cousin had spruced up our ancestral home, installing new plumbing, new wiring, and new tatami floors. One evening, several days after our arrival, he dropped in and presented my father with the bill.

"But, Dad," I protested, "you didn't ask for the repairs. You didn't sign any contracts. There's no reason whatsoever for the bill. I would refuse to pay it."

"Hold on, said my father, I don't know whether I am supposed to pay this bill or not. Perhaps it is just a way to show me how much the repairs cost. It's all right, son, don't you worry about it. Either I am meant only to see the costs of the repairs or, my cousin feels the bill will not be a hardship for me. So, you see, either way, it's all right."

I couldn't understand how such a simple thing could become so convoluted, and I told my father that there was "no way I could live in this crazy country."

As it turned out, the bill was not meant to be paid. I asked my father what had made him suspect that the bill was not for him.

"It's the way the bill was presented," my father said. "Kenji didn't stay to see me open the envelope. If he had expected me to pay the bill, he would have waited."

It was all somewhat mysterious to me, but not all communications are rendered in print, and some gestures are certainly more powerful than any words. Perhaps it was not only my mother who relied on the unspoken word, the implied suggestion. In any case, this incident was yet another reminder that one cannot be both fish and fowl. In order to truly understand the people of my ancestry, I would have had to live in Japan. There was no other way to do it.

The party my father's "cousin" hosted was unlike any other I have ever attended. The guests were all men, with the exception of a few women who represented their "male-deprived" families. We all knelt on soft cushions before a low, black lacquered table, with each place setting having been meticulously laid. Elaborate, colorful dishes, some steamed, some fried and still others baked or broiled, were paraded before us. Hot sake was poured into large bowls, and each guest bowed in front of my brother and me, the honoured guests. In this sexist country my sister was not accorded the same respect. We were expected to pick up the bowl in both hands, shout "kampai" and drink the hot sake in one gulp. Before long, many men turned red in the face and others tottered from their sitting positions. Then, a karaoke machine was brought out, and every guest, regardless of his sobriety or ability to perform, had to sing a short tune. The display was at best, embarrassing, both for the performer and the listener. My brother and I were amazed that we were able to tolerate the alcohol better than the natives, many of them now prostrate on the tatami floor. When the party ended in the wee hours of the night, each guest was sent home with a wheelbarrow full of gifts, each one elaborately wrapped. It was an amazing introduction to a culture that was both foreign and strangely captivating at the same time.

My second trip to Japan occurred in October, 1989. I was selected by the chairman of the meeting, the Kyoto professor of Urology, Dr. Osamu

Yoshida, to deliver a paper and to co-chair a session at The Seventh International Endourology Meeting in Kyoto. He liked my book, *"Private Parts"*, which had been published in 1988, and he undertook to publish the Japanese version of it. I cannot judge the merits of the Japanese translation, but I can describe how the book was made. Professor Yoshida assigned different pages of the book for translation by members of his faculty, and the compiled text was then edited by people working for the publishing house. Although I cannot read the Japanese text, I am certain that the flow of the material must have been affected by the fact that there were so many translators involved. Dr. Yoshida confided to me that he discouraged the publishers from playing

With Dr. Osamu Yoshida, professor of Urology, Kyoto, who was responsible for the Japanese version of **Private Parts**

up the sexual aspects of the book, such as the management of impotence, the emphasis on which, might have enhanced its sale; however, the fact that there were ten thousand copies printed, gave me cause for great satisfaction. Parenthetically, I also wondered if the Japanese edition of my book had been published, not because of any inherent merit of the product, but because the Kyoto professor, a powerful figure, had deemed it appropriate.

Mr. Taro Ichikawa, a middle management executive from Kodansha, made a three hour train trip from Tokyo to Kyoto just to meet me. I felt flattered and spent some time with him at a party which celebrated the successful conclusion of the international meeting. Eventually, Dr. Yoshida came to my side and asked me why I was spending so much time with a "common businessman" with whom I was involved in polite conversation. I gathered that as an academic, it was not the proper allocation of my energy. I was struck with this contrast in attitude with that of the west, where he who pays the piper, is rewarded by the attention. It is yet another example of the way in which attitude and political connections sometimes take precedence over learning and scientific truth.

I believe that scientific papers are sometimes published due to the reputation of the lead author, and that government research grants may be allocated in similar fashion. Early in my career I had reviewed papers on behalf of my chief. I was given subtle instructions to be generous in my assessment because the paper had come from a centre which would be reviewing our own efforts. On another occasion, a paper I had submitted for publication, was rejected. My chief called me to his office and asked me if the paper had merit. I told him I believed it to be a solid, original work. He made a few phone calls and the paper was subsequently published. So much for fairness and excellence in the scientific community! In recent years I have been asked to referee papers submitted to our national medical journal. Almost invariably, I have suggested acceptance, with perhaps, a few minor alterations; and almost as invariably, the papers are rejected by the other referees. "Not original enough!" "Similar data published elsewhere!" "Not suitable for a national publication!" are some of the more common negative comments given by the other referees. I wonder why we are so stringent about acceptance when, at the same time, we allow other statements with neither editorial input nor scientific validity to flood the internet? While I realize we have no control over this medium, it rankles, nonetheless.

I had thought of spending a sabbatical period in Japan in the company of Dr. Yoshida and his associates, but I eventually decided against it because I could not persuade my wife to participate in the adventure, and because my finances would have taken a beating. During a sabbatical period I could have collected my university salary, but the bulk of my income was then derived from clinical practice. In retrospect, I should have taken the sabbatical. It is one of the few regrets I have in my lifetime — of opportunities offered and declined. Dr. Yoshida's words "This is the house we picked out for you," pointing to a handsome cottage not far from the university hospital, still invade my mind in those quiet moments when I ponder the past. I find it interesting that in life, regrets are reserved for things left undone, rather than for things done, even if they were done poorly, even badly.

Dr. Yusaka Okada, the professor of Urology in Shiga-ken and an associate of Dr. Yoshida, was exceptionally kind to me, perhaps in part, because his wife had come from the same prefecture as my parents. He invited me and my son to dinner at his home and it was an exceptional treat. Later in the evening, I asked Dr. Okada how much he earned in a year. He evaded the question, but I persisted and he finally told me that he made "X" yen as salary. Looking at his beautiful home, his car, his daughters' private school and his out-of-country trips, I told him that "it just didn't add up."

"Well ... actually, when we treat wealthy patients, they supplement our income with an envelope under the table," he confessed.

Dr. Okada was also my guest in Montreal, and I invited him to attend our regular rounds. He had no hesitation expressing his medical opinion, in halting English, even when he was taking a minority stance, and he often confessed his ignorance, when faced with a new medical situation. He endeared himself to the entire gathering.

I could have worked with Yusaka Okada for the period of my sabbatical. He was forthright and candid; rare traits in the native Japanese! It is with some regret that I believe that many Japanese are not forthright. In keeping with age-old traditions, they would bear a grudge than be openly critical. Candor is uncomfortable for them, and often, subterfuge will often substitute for the truth. This may be a trait which has been inculcated into the society at large; however, it is my hope that the next generations will see a more emotionally honest individual emerging from this crowded, island society.

On that particular trip to Japan, I was accompanied by my son who was at a crossroads in his life, wondering what he should do, now that he was twenty-five years old and had concentrated on Philosophy and Kierkegaard, as his field of study. He decided to spend more time in Japan and didn't return with me. He has never regretted the time he spent away although he was brutal in his assessment of the Japanese. "They are like ants," he said, "industrious, determined, and highly focused on their tasks, but they never stop to wonder what it's all about." I thought it was an astute observation, although I'm not so sure it applies to the entire population. It is a fact that the Japanese, unlike the American, does not want to draw attention to himself. "The nail that sticks out is the one that will be struck" is a frequently repeated adage. This reluctance to "stick out" may be endearing, but can be mistaken for a lack of confidence.

At about this time we (my sister, brother and I) decided to give away our ancestral home to a cousin. The house had been built by my grandfather, passed on to my father, and then to me as the eldest son. We held a family conference. I had no more right to it than my sister or my brother, but as all three of us were thriving in Canada, we thought we should relinquish ownership of the property while my mother was alive and well. I made a trip to the Japanese consulate in Montreal with my mother, and she explained what we wanted to do. Apparently, I had to indicate in my own handwriting that I wished to

Our ancestral home which we gave away to our cousin

pass on the property to Hajime Kawasaki, my cousin. The problem was that I could not write Japanese. No problem — I simply had to copy the document supplied. I spent the next few hours trying to copy the script. It was like duplicating art-work. The Japanese official was, to say the least, bemused. Eventually, I passed over a sheet of paper that made no sense to me and which was probably totally illegible to him. Nevertheless, this appeared to fulfil the legal requirement for the transfer of property, and in due time, the transaction was completed; thus severing yet another link to the ancient country.

My third trip to Japan took place in 1995. The international pharmaceutical firm, Schering, sent me to Thailand and Pakistan to talk about how we manage prostate cancer in Canada. This time I was accompanied on the trip by my second daughter, Jocelyn. She had earned a D.Phil in Chemistry from Oxford and had some time on her hands before she commenced work in the pharma-ceutical industry. We detoured to Japan first, to see Carolin, our youngest daughter, who was stationed in Ishino-maki, on the northern shore of Honshu. Carolin, like many Canadian university graduates was in Japan, teaching English. I saw with my own eyes that our little girl was a big hit in the little coastal town. While relating some of her more interesting stories to us, she explained that above all, she had to take great care with her words. Once she had admired a suit worn by one of her mature students. Then and there, the lady wanted to take

it off and give it to her. When my daughter protested vehemently, the lady understood. She sent
the dry cleaned suit to her apartment the next day.
There were many such gestures of generosity –
making every social occasion an excuse for gift-
giving, and whenever my daughter offered a token
gift in exchange, it was used as an excuse for
another gift. "It was totally embarrassing," my
daughter said.

We had a most enjoyable stay, highlighted by a
surprise welcome party in our honour, and a visit
to a park not far from the school, made special by
a statue of Basho, the famous Zen Haiku poet. Here
is one of his most famous haikus:

Furu ike ya The old pond
Kawazu tobikomu, A frog jumps in,
Mizu no oto. The water's sound!

The three line poem, with its mandatory five-
seven-five syllables, seems simple, child-like, and
yet it is profound. The image and the sound
intrude upon our consciousness and linger.

In counterpoint to this most beautiful poem, I
recall one jarring note. We had to travel within the
country by train and the people working for the
railways were curt and unpleasant. I asked a man
for instructions and was told to consult the big
board. When I said I had difficulty with that, he
looked at me, assessed me as not being worthy of
his help, and turned away. (I was not as clever as
one of my Japanese-Canadian friends who said he
had difficulty with the board because he had
forgotten his glasses.) On one platform I was told to

go in one direction by one man, and in exactly the opposite direction by another. As a rule, the people who did not know I was a "visiting professor" treated me with total disdain.

The people in Pakistan and Thailand, however, treated me wonderfully well, but I was distressed to discover the cancer treatments they wanted me to talk about were cutting-edge, and very expensive, a distressing fact, because the country was filled with the poor and the needy. This disparity made it all the more difficult to deliver my address, as I realized that only a tiny percentage of the population would ever benefit from the quality of these medical drugs and procedures. This was particularly striking in Pakistan. I saw grown men fighting over the right to carry our luggage, limbless children begging outside our air-conditioned limousine, and critically ill patients brought to the hospital on piggy-back and in wheel barrows.

I was introduced to a radio-oncologist who told me that Pakistan had purchased a nuclear reactor from Canada, but that when Canada refused to service the broken reactor, they had to learn to make the repairs themselves. He proudly implied that they could not only carry out the repairs but they could also make nuclear bombs. I wondered the point of becoming a nuclear power if you could not provide the bare necessities of life for your citizens.

In Thailand, gold trimmings adorned the many palaces, while downtown traffic was log-jammed everywhere. The native guides were very careful with their remarks. Any negative comments about the royal family could lead to dangerous repercussions, I was told. I developed a new appreciation for Canada.

My fourth trip to Japan took place in 1998. This time I was supported in large measure by the pharmaceutical firm, Astra-Zeneca. I was scheduled to lecture in six cities, at universities scattered across the country. My wife again declined to go, so I took my 87 year old mother. When my hosts heard that I was bringing my mother, they were more troubled than they admitted to me in their communications. Upon our arrival, they had an ambulance, a stretcher, and a wheel-chair ready, just in case. We were treated like royalty. The Japanese respect teachers and the elderly, and my mother and I matched that particular combination to a tee. I was considered "oya-koko," which meant someone kind to his parents and worthy of extra regard. In every city my hosts tried to outdo the kindness of the previous site.

Our itinerary took us from Tokyo to Yokohama, then to Nagoya, Matsumoto, Kyoto, and, finally, to Yonago city, in Tottori-ken. My plan was simple. At each site I planned to show the one hour documentary on prostate cancer I had the privilege of making for Galafilm. It was called: *"Prostate Cancer: the Male Nightmare."*

The documentary follows three of my patients after they are diagnosed with prostate cancer. One man chooses surgery and the camera follows him into the operating room; the second man has

hormones and radiotherapy and the camera shows
him receiving radiotherapy and injecting the drug
under his skin. The third man is exploring alternative treatments to the standard hormone
injections, and the camera follows him into his
kitchen cupboard packed full of dietary
supplements. It also documents his visit to an
acupuncturist, a meditation expert, and an exercise
guru. After each screening, I had planned to open
up the subject for a general discussion. Among the
unexpected surprises I discovered was the fact that
it is illegal for anyone other than a doctor to inject
any product into a human body in Japan. What a
clever way to curb illicit drug use, I thought. I
suppose addicts can steal syringes and drugs and
illegally inject themselves – but it is one added
deterrent. Here in Canada, the laws regarding
injection appear to be more relaxed, so that the
number of individuals who can walk into a
pharmacy and buy syringes, is far greater than it is
in Japan.

I have treasured memories from each city. In
Yokohama, we were the guests of Teruaki Iwamoto.
He is the chief of Urology at St. Marianna
University, and has built a reputation relating
environmental "hormones" to the declining sperm
counts in Japan. St. Marianna is a private medical
school and its former dean was the late Dr. Eizo
Toguri, a Japanese-Canadian. Eizo was the oldest of
a remarkable family. The youngest sibling is my
friend, Allan, a Canadian urologist, practicing in
Toronto. On my first visit to Japan, Allan arranged

for me to meet his oldest brother and I was treated to a most remarkable evening in Tokyo. Dean Toguri asked me what I wanted to do, and I replied that I wanted to see an authentic geisha. I did not know that this form of entertainment had become obsolete in Tokyo but his young associates took me to its modern equivalent. I was treated to a costly lobster dinner and a stage show. I thought the evening was over, when I was escorted to a back room. Attractive young Japanese ladies promptly sat down beside me. They were dressed in fashionable western outfits, not kimonos, and wore lip-stick and eye liners; not the exaggerated white-flour-like make-up of the geisha. They were charming and spoke glowingly of my very limited command of Japanese, as they kept the whiskey glass set before me filled to the top. One of the girls had an acceptable command of English.

"You are an attractive young lady," I said to her, "Don't you want to get married and raise a family rather than to be spending your evenings in a place like this?"

"You think I should get married and stay at home while my husband enjoys himself at places like this?" she replied. (As James Thurber said in his version of the Little Red Riding Hood story: "Then, she pulled out a hand gun from her basket and shot the wolf dead," adding the moral: "Little girls are not as naive as they used to be.")

Yokohama and St. Marianna were a return, for me, to favored sites. The conference itself was made memorable by an expert translator who did not stumble once, translating my English into impeccable Japanese. It was a shame, I mused later, that her command of the two languages was so much better than that of the health professionals I had encountered in Japan. With all the advances being made in medicine, and published in English journals these days, better courses in English, especially spoken English, would be of benefit to Japanese medical students.

In Nagoya, I met a young urologist who had done his post-graduate studies in Vancouver. He was among the authors of an important scientific publication which first suggested merit in administering hormones on an intermittent schedule, for patients with prostate cancer. I wanted to ask him if the idea had come from him or from his research supervisors, but I missed the opportunity. I was distracted by Dr. Gotoh, who had spent time with us in Montreal and was probably responsible for my invitation there.

The lead author of a scientific paper is the person largely responsible for the statement or hypothesis put forward, and there can be heated arguments regarding the order in which the names of the authors should appear. It's also amusing to me that the media and the public often get the allocation of merit all wrong. Recently, for example, there was a newspaper story that cited Thomas Stamey. The Stanford urologist had claimed that the PSA blood test was useless in diagnosing early prostate cancer. A number of patients came to me with the clipping and asked if it was true that "the man who invented the blood test now said it was ineffective." I pointed out that Tom Stamey is a giant figure in Urology, but that he was not the inventor the PSA blood test. In fact, the protein was discovered by Hara, a Japanese scientist, who called it gamma seminoprotein. It was named PSA (Prostate Specific Antigen) by Wang and associates working at Roswell Park, Buffalo, and popularized as a potentially useful test by Stamey first, and then by Catalona, and others. The PSA was never the gold standard test to help make the initial diagnosis of prostate cancer, but for monitoring the disease, it is the single best marker we have in all of medicine. Furthermore, PSA changes over time is a very helpful criterion in selecting men who should undergo biopsy.

In Matsumoto, I was the guest of Osamu Nishizawa. "Sam" had spent time in studies at McGill and we had become friends. At the Urology meeting in Anaheim, California, in June 2001, I invited him and his wife to share dinner at a Japanese restaurant with urologists from Quebec. As dinner ended, Sam got up and said he wanted to sing a song in appreciation. None of the Canadians understood the lyrics, of course, but we were all impressed with the gesture and with the performance.

In Kyoto, my friends Osamu Yoshida and Yusaka Okada went out of their way to make our trip the best ever to Japan. At one party, the beer label had my picture on it. At another reception in a famous restaurant, the elaborate dinner was served as we sat facing a moonlit sky. The view is one cherished by generations of Japanese patrons, who have burst out in Haiku. Generations of royalty, noblemen, and samurai have been enthralled by this setting, I was told. I felt a sense of history, and felt my eyes moisten. It appears that I have a connection with Japan, which goes deeper than the merely intellectual.

At the conference itself, which was exceptionally well attended, I asked one of the young doctors if he had been ordered to attend or had come of his own volition and interest. He only smiled. I strongly suspected all the young doctors had been instructed to attend and I wondered what their fate would have been had they failed to do so. It also gave me the chance to reassess my reputation as a seasoned speaker.

In Yonago, I was the guest of two more doctors who had done post-graduate training in Montreal. Dr Miyagawa, the professor, and his young associate, Dr. Hirakawa were not going to be outdone by Kyoto. We were treated to a grand tour of the area and booked into a luxury hotel set in a hot spring. Because the ceiling was made of a gigantic glass plate, I could see stars twinkling in the distant skies as I soaked in the hot spring water. It was quite an up-grade from the bathhouses in the war camp and I could not help thinking about the comparison as I juxtaposed the images.

It's interesting to me that three of our four children have sought out Japan as a place to visit and explore. Our oldest daughter, Kathleen, is the only one who has yet to make the trip. But, she is anxious to go.

I was invited to meet a Japanese professor of orthopedic surgery at the home of *nikkei* friends, Bob and Joy Kadowaki. They were hosting the professor because their daughter, Linda, had met him while she was teaching English in Japan after having completed her undergraduate degree at the University of Western Ontario.

The professor was to present a paper at a prestigious conference, and he was far from happy with his delivery. He asked if I would be kind enough to hear him speak, and to react. The fine meal and good company had done their work and I agreed. Seeing my almost constant frown during his delivery, unnerved him as much as speaking to a huge audience, and he stopped to ask what was wrong. I explained that the translator he had used

My children, Kathleen, Carolin, Edwin, and Jocelyn clowning around in their university sweat shirts (1989)

was not competent in that area; so much so, that his speech was barely acceptable at best. After a few hours, however, we had him "back on track".

"It may not be a prize-winning paper but the point you are trying to make is clearer now," I said.

"I hope it's not too clear," said the professor, "because, then, they'll ask me questions."

I should note that one of the pet peeves I have with Japanese doctors and scientists is the fact that their presentations at international conferences seem almost apologetic. Surely, with all the work they have done to amass the data and prepare the papers, they can avail themselves of better coaching on how to spruce up their deliveries.

My journeys to the "old country" have awakened in me, a sense of belonging, accompanied by a great sense of regret. While Canada is, and will always be my country, I would have liked to have examined the roots of the great heritage from which I came. My childhood ambivalence about 'belonging' has been settled in my mind, but I would still like to extend my association with the country of my ancestors.

Picture of our four children, Edwin, Carolin, Kathleen, and Jocelyn (1991)

China and other locations

I had been invited to serve as part of an international faculty for a medical symposium to take place in Beijing, China, in 1982. I agreed to participate, provided I could detour to Japan, en route, since the timing coincided perfectly with the family reunion I described earlier.

The medical symposium was simply a clever deal put together by an enterprising American businessman. China was just beginning to open its doors to foreign tourists, and an international faculty could be enticed to make the trip at the prospect of an expense-covered deal. Doctors and their spouses from across North America might sign up because the symposium aspect made the trip, in large measure, tax deductible, and the organizers could profit from the post-symposium tour of five cities within China, which was an integral part of the package.

I was struck by the splendor of Hong Kong and the abject poverty in China... at that time. No nation can prosper, I thought, if it stifles dissent and locks up its intellectuals. One man on a tractor mower tilled a family farm in Japan. The same work was done by a dozen men with picks and shovels in China. I had little doubt in my mind though that when the dormant giant eventually stirred, the world was going to wake up to a formidable nation. There was nothing wrong with the geography of the land, nor with the intelligence or industry of its people. It was simply inevitable that a nation on bicycles would switch to automobiles, and that construction cranes would replace the bamboo scaffolding. In fact, by the turn of the century, eighty percent of the construction cranes known to be operating in the world, were in China.

I wondered if it was an oriental trait to be oppressed by a ruling class; that is to say, the military in Japan and the communist leaders in China. It was intriguing that the populace, brighter than the leaders, allowed so much power to be concentrated in the hands of so few. I considered at length, the parallels with Germany, Italy and Russia, but the only conclusion I could draw, only returned me to the fact that power is a potent aphrodisiac; one that men will not easily relinquish. It is a universal, and not an oriental trait, it seems.

There are few modest and saintly political rulers.

I have had the good fortune to attend medical conferences all over the world. It was only in Japan, though, that I felt a connection to the land and its people. I was not surprised to discover that the hospitals in Japan were spotless, but distressed to learn that the number of people employed to keep them clean and tidy was one third the number of those employed at my hospital in Montreal, although the number of beds was comparable. I saw fascinating geography in many other countries but I did not see enough of the land nor its people to make an accurate comment or judgement. I discovered, instead, how easily I could be fooled. In Brazil, I was entertained by a fortune teller. The matronly native woman threw some shells on the table-top and announced that I was involved in a major project involving words. "It will be a success," she proclaimed. As I was working on a book-in-progress at the time I thought her skills unbelievable and truly remarkable. When I spoke about it to a friend at home he put me straight. "Do you know of any project that doesn't involve words?" he asked.

My Father

I don't know anyone who has taken a belief in Christianity more seriously or more passionately than my father. He embraced Christianity's basic tenets and their application to life; thus he disapproved of lying, swearing, cheating, drinking, and gambling. This good man lived an exemplary, almost saintly life. He had his lapses, to be sure but, overall, he could be counted as a very moral individual. His epiphany, which he likened to the conversion of Paul on the road to Damascus, occurred early in life, as a youth in Canada. He kept this encounter with the Almighty to himself, because he never revealed the details to me. I wish I had asked him about it. Was he anti-Christian, like Paul, for example, before his conversion? Did he feel that he had to abandon Buddhism in order to become a Christian? Was it difficult for him to do so?

Unfortunately, in life, it is only in hindsight that we become aware of lost opportunities, and this one is irretrievable. Suffice it to say that, once imbued with the spirit of the Christian faith, my father found comfort, strength and peace for the rest of his life; to the extent that even his passing was marked by a strong and binding attachment to the Almighty.

The man who directed my father into the Christian faith was a Reverend Akagawa, a Harvard man, and the pastor who serviced our town, as well as many other Japanese-Canadian communities in the Fraser Valley of British Columbia, before World War II. As a young child, I knew the United Church minister, and met him again when I was twelve years old, when our family relocated to Quebec. It was the summer of 1946, and he met us at the railway station in Winnipeg. All I recall of that journey though is how unbearably hot it was on that train, and how good a cold glass of water could taste. We were booked on a "coach" car and we were fixed to our seats for four seemingly endless days. (Years later I made the same trip in a sleeper car and realized how comfortable a train trip could be, given the right conditions.)

Reverend Akagawa was like most men of the cloth – self-assured, engaging, polite, and fatherly. He was a welcome, although understated part of my youth. The more charismatic pastor was a Reverend McWilliams, a United Church minister and missionary, who volunteered to service us during the war years, when we were confined to the detention camp in interior British Columbia. I thought it strange that a giant white man could speak Japanese so effortlessly, as well as enjoy a hot bowl of rice. "If you chew it long enough the rice turns sweet," I remember him saying.

Although simple in nature, these words have recurred to me on those occasions when I am ready to make a hasty, negative judgement. It is interesting, the way in which words from one's past sometimes serve as unannounced beacons in later years.

My father persuaded my mother to join the church, and the children had no choice. We attended service every week without fail, dressed always in our Sunday best. I hated that. My neck chafed from the starched collar of the white shirt, and the polished black shoes were stiff and not suitable for running off into the bushes, nor for kicking rocks and cans as I wished to do. I couldn't get out of my going-to-church outfit quickly enough.

I was christened at a Christmas service before I started kindergarten. My parents neglected to warn me what was in store, so when I saw some kind of liquid splashed onto the heads of the nominees, I panicked. I ran from the altar as fast as my feet could take me, knocking over the Christmas tree in my panicky flight. I still remember the crash; the whooshing, slow-motion tumbling of the giant fir, and the collective gasp from the congregation. I don't know if my parents were ever asked to pay for damages, but their weekly contribution to the collection was always very generous and totally disproportionate to my father's income.

In Montreal, after the war, because the community did not have its own church, we borrowed facilities from the Ukranian United Church on Amherst street. Eventually, the Japanese-Canadian congregation bought a house with an adjoining empty lot and built its own house of worship. My father was one of the founding members and was proud of his role. Home gatherings, though, continued, and our house was always the locale for the congregation of church members. The modest dwelling my father purchased in Montreal was picked, I am certain, because the wall dividing the dining room from the living room could be opened up to create one large room appropriate for the congregation of the faithful. These home gatherings, known as "katei-shukai," were occasions for the singing of hymns, gospel reading, sermons from the minister and speeches from selected members. I don't know if the speakers were pre-selected and came with prepared talks, or simply spoke from their hearts, but nobody who spoke ever stumbled. I was always impressed with that. Meetings bordered on the evangelical, but there were never any cries of "hallelujah!" The gathering ended with a feast which was partly pot-luck but largely host-concocted. I don't know if the people came for the spiritual nourishment or for the food, but I suspect the latter, as my mother had a reputation for being an exceptionally gifted cook. Her maki-sushi, chow-mein, and manju (sweet red beans enclosed within a sticky rice wrapping) were acknowledged as "out of this world", a not unreasonable term for church-cooking.

My father often took on the role of "substitute minister" when the pastor was away. He led the congregation in readings of the scripture and he delivered the equivalent of a sermon. As his son, I felt he could even perform the baptismal rites or wedding ceremonies if he had wanted to do so. Pride was only one of the myriad emotions I felt for this amazing man.

I didn't appreciate how deeply my father held his faith until our time together in Japan, at a family gathering in October, 1982. Remarkably, this revelation had nothing to do with the church, and everything to do with earth and rice. He took me for a walk to visit a neighbour and, when we had gone half-way, he stopped dead in his tracks and asked me to look around. I did exactly as I was told, and in every direction, as far as my eyes could see, were rice fields, the golden autumn crop undulating in the breeze. In fact, they reminded me of the wheat fields I had seen in the Canadian prairies, when the train had brought us east.

My father asked me to tell him what I saw, and of course, I said "Rice fields."

It was then that he told me the land had been ours, before the war. The Japanese government had seized it and parceled it out to the local residents. I looked at the vast acreage and wondered aloud if my father was upset at the loss.

"Son," he said, "look again. See how well the rice is growing, how well the fields are being tended. The government was right to take it away."

I was astonished by my father's remark, and my respect for him rose another notch. I could not understand why anybody could be so accepting of government thievery. I would have clamored for appropriate compensation. My father accepted the manner in which the Japanese government treated him, in the same way he accepted the Canadian government's mistreatment. I attributed it to his Christian faith. It was to me, Christ-like.

I had difficulty accepting my father's final illness. It simply did not reflect the man himself. He was thin and wiry all his life and never sick. He found energy after a hard day's work to make and maintain a vegetable garden, no matter where we lived; in fact, he made one on the mountain slopes in Tashme (the detention camp where we were confined during the war years) and claimed squatter's rights to a spot below the high tension wires near our house in east-end Montreal, just north of the city's Botanical Gardens. His gardens thrived no matter where, because he worked the soil so lovingly. Leftovers from supper, spoiled vegetables, peels from potatoes, apples and oranges, and even egg shells, were carefully worked into the soil, long before I had ever heard of compost. Stones and pebbles were sifted out and piled neatly in one corner; and eventually, dark soil replaced sand and clay. In the fall, the soil was turned over once again in preparation for the following year. He never tired of working the garden and he never complained about the effort it required. It was his way.

The only time he could not go to work nor tend his garden was when he almost cut off his left forearm with a power-saw at work. (It is a work ethic I must have inherited, because in almost forty years of medical practice I have never taken a day off because of illness.) My father's job was to cut the long lumber into more manageable pieces for the manufacture of bedroom sets. On the day of his injury he was trying to do more than the usual quota of work because he was planning to ask for a day off to attend my brother's graduation from McGill's Faculty of Medicine. He severed several blood vessels and tendons, and although he recovered quickly from surgery, he had to wear an above-elbow plaster cast for a while, and his left arm never functioned properly afterward. He was always rubbing it with his good hand. Over time, his left hand became disfigured, and his ring and little finger remained closed, locked into that position for the remainder of his life. He never had any heart ailment, nor any of the debilitating neurological disorders which victimized so many of his friends. But, he could not escape cancer.

It was now 1984. An earlier diagnosis of stomach cancer was missed because the barium meal X-ray had been read inaccurately, and now my father lay in a hospital bed recovering from an operation simply to by-pass a blockage. His disease was beyond curative surgery.

"Hand me my bible," he said to me.

I reached into the drawer of a side table beside his hospital bed and passed him his precious dog-eared King James' version. He opened its faded yellow pages at random and read a passage in silence. He said it was a segment in which St. Paul describes a trip over rough water. The voyage would be difficult but he would survive. My father took that to mean he had a chance. I rejoiced at a faith that could comfort a man to such a degree.

Years later I searched for the passage. I found it in Acts 27:

I now bid you take heart, for there will be no loss of life among you, but only of the ship.

For this very night there stood by me an angel of the God to whom I belong and whom I worship, and he said, "Do not be afraid, Paul; you must stand before Caesar; and lo, God has granted you all those who sail with you."

In my own life, I have yet to find the depth of comfort that these passages gave to my late father. It is a legacy to which I still aspire, without the certainty that I will achieve this goal.

Months after the bible episode, when my father knew he was terminal, and was being cared for at my brother's house in Kingston, Ontario, he planned his own funeral. "It must be a celebration," he said, "for a life fully lived." Indeed, this remarkable man lived a full life, and when the time came, we celebrated, as was fitting of this patriarch's wonderful existence here on earth. It was a tribute to a man, who had as his standard, an abiding faith in the goodness of man, and an unbreakable bond with a loving, caring God. No one could have asked for a finer model for emulation.

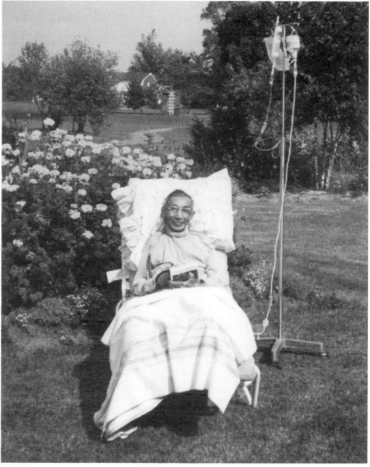

*My father at my brother's home in Kingston
shortly before his death*

Religion

I find it remarkable that Christianity, a religion based on a leap of faith, should consider charity more important than faith or hope. *"And now abideth faith, hope, and charity, but the greatest of these is charity,"* declared Paul. The idea of "giving till it hurts" makes sense, and the aphorism that whatever you give will be returned to you many times over, has proven itself again and again.

Devout members of some Christian denominations donate ten percent of their income to the church. I know a doctor friend, a member of the Salvation Army, who does exactly that. He is not poorer for it. There is a virtue in charity.

My father taught me the meaning of this attribute, not from any stern lecture, but by his actions. He first gave away his land and then, as much as he could afford it, he gave to his church Other people must have recognized his charitable nature, but some still thought that a well-earned eulogy could be bought. I remember an elderly couple who tried to endear themselves to my parents, and visited frequently, bearing gifts. When my father, suspecting something, asked them the reason for their largesse, they replied simply and honestly that they were getting older, and wanted him to say some kind words about them at their funerals. I supposed everybody wanted something decent said at their funerals, but I didn't know that people could actually cultivate it. The eulogy for my father was delivered by his friend and fellow church elder, a Mr. Yukio Niiya. "I cannot get out of my head the image of Mr. Taguchi slaving endless hours to produce Japanese noodles for the church bazaar," he said. The bazaar was a major source of income for the church, and the noodle servings made a significant contribution. It had a secret recipe, a gift from a lonely man my parents had befriended before the war. At bazaar time, every year, I was reminded that my father's contribution was due in part, to a gift from another individual.

It was during our war-time confinement, 1943, when I realized that not all people were Christians. In fact, many Japanese-Canadians, including my own relatives, were Buddhists, worshiping differently in what they called a "temple" instead of a church. They congregated like the Christians on Sunday, but their service involved chanting, the clapping of boards, and the clanging of bells. Throughout most of the service the worshipers had their eyes closed and their hands held up in prayer, while rosaries dangled from their hands. I was never forbidden to attend a Buddhist service but I had come to believe that it would be a sin to do so. Curiosity got the better of me, however, and one afternoon, I sneaked into a Buddhist service. I thought I was committing a mortal sin. The experience was frightening, exhilarating, captivating, and boring – all at once! Although I did not realize it, this experience, and my childhood friendship with a Buddhist buddy, would return to shape me in later years. Suffice it to say that my theology in those years was made up of more questions than answers; a fact that has not really changed to this day, as I live the experiences of every passing year and see the despair, the pain and the misunderstanding which exists in our world.

The Christians and the Buddhists at the internment camp were often at loggerheads. Each side did not have a whole lot of respect for the other. It was not outright contempt but there was an unmistakable disdain evident between the groups. The Christians, I think, felt they were the more well adapted, the more modern, and the more in tune with the country to which they had come. The Buddhists, on the other hand, felt they were the more respectful of their roots and felt that the Christians had forsaken that fundamental essential. The members of the community had to be one or the other in order to gain acceptance. Being both was out of the question, although sometimes, a person switched allegiances, to the chagrin of his friends.

I could not fathom why the community was divided into the two camps, nor why the two were so discrete and incompatible. I thought every child should clamor to be a Christian and get presents from Santa Claus.

Many hymns at our service were sung to the same tune in English and in Japanese by the entire congregation. "Hymn number sixty in English and number forty-four in Japanese," the minister would call out. I wondered if the translations were accurate, I didn't think that was likely because songs other than hymns did not have literal translations. As one example, the first line of Auld Lang Syne, "Should auld acquaintance be forgot..." was sung in Japanese as Hotaru no hikari... "By the light of the fireflies"... hardly a literal translation, although the melody was the same.

Readings from the bible, whether by the minister or by a member of the congregation though, were moving experiences. Was not Jesus speaking of the Japanese-Canadians when he said: "Blessed are you when men hate you, and ostracize you, and insult you, and scorn your name as evil?"

But some of His teachings did not reflect the reality of life. Who actually turned the other cheek when he was hit? Why should the meek inherit the world? Why should it be more difficult for a rich man to enter Heaven than for a camel to go through the eye of a needle?

Furthermore, and these arguments came to me later, why were Christians so hung up on the question of a virgin birth, the betrayal, the crucifixion, and the return to life after death? Why dwell on these points which seemed to me inconsequential and which detracted from the real teachings of Christ: "Love thy neighbor. Do good to those who hate you. Bless those who curse you. Pray for those who mistreat you."

The trouble with Christianity seems to be that every Christian pays lip-service to it, but very few Christians I knew, other than my father, ever practiced it fully, and with a whole heart. Misfortunes never shook my father's faith in God, and he was always charitable. But, I could never be as devout.

My friend, an orthopedic surgeon, just starting a promising career was struck down with pancreatic cancer. My colleague with whom I had trained, developed Lou Gehrig's disease. Both died prematurely. Why would God allow this? If we are God's children, isn't He our Father? What parent would treat his own children that way? "One anguished cry of a child negates the concept of God," said Friedrich Nietzsche. It was an argument I couldn't refute, and I am still wrestling with the conceptual reality of a world of pain and a God of love.

I was well into middle age when I once again, became curious about Buddhism. I investigated the four noble truths and the eightfold paths. Surprisingly, they did not seem very distant from the ten commandments, nor the sermon on the mount. I searched for a reason why a person could not be a Buddhist and a Christian concurrently, and I couldn't find it. "God is Love," says Christianity. "Hatreds never cease by hatreds in this world. By love alone they cease," says Buddhism. Christianity has adopted the Ten Commandments: Buddhism promotes the Five Precepts; forbidding killing, theft, adultery, lying, and intoxication. Christianity has its enigmatic Trinity: God the Father, God the Son, God the Holy Spirit. Buddhism speaks of its three treasures, Buddha, the peaceful perfection, Dharma, the true teaching, and Samgha, the true brotherhood but, like the holy trinity, the three treasures seem to mystify rather than to clarify.

The four noble truths Buddhism espoused are as follows: Life is suffering. The cause of suffering is desire. Overcome the desire and it is possible to banish the suffering. The way to do that is by adopting the eightfold pathways. These were: the right aspiration, the right action, the right understanding, the right speech, the right livelihood, the right effort, the right concentration, and the right mindfulness.

Where was the incompatibility? Why couldn't a Buddhist adopt the teachings of Christ if he wished? Why couldn't a Christian follow the eightfold paths if he wished?

And then, I discovered Zen. I found the writings of Daisetz T. Suzuki fascinating and I found the Zen koan intriguing. There were anecdotes Suzuki told that tickled my fancy but which did not satisfy my scientific training. Let me mention just one example. Suzuki tells a story of a legendary sword-smith of the Kamakura period (1185-1338) by the name of Okazaki Masamune, whose ablest pupil, Muramasa made swords with edges so sharp that when one was placed in a current of water, dead leaves coming into its path were cut sharply in two. But, according to the legend, when the Masamune sword was substituted in its place, the leaves avoided the sword.

What can be made of this legend? Is it suggesting that the leaves avoided the sharper blade out of respect? Or, can we describe a blade to be sharper than the sharpest – by ascribing to it another dimension? Can we be better-than-best? Is morality time and place-limited? I also asked myself why an inanimate object, like a dead leaf, should be given the power of volition, when we, as human beings, often lack the ability to plot our own life-courses.

On first hearing the story, I had an emotional response. What a satisfying tale; akin to Jesus feeding the multitude with a few fish, or raising Lazarus from his tomb.

Zen, I found, is not a panacea for all the problems that afflict mankind. It does not even try to compete with other religions in explaining creation, the supernatural, or after death experiences; however, it does deal with life and existence, in a remarkably introspective way

As a way of training us, it also offers us situations which are difficult for the mind to grasp. How can I listen to the sound of one hand clapping, or picture my original face before my parents were born? These are the Zen koans and they can be upsetting because they challenge our customary way of thinking.

The secret, which might readily be explained, is not so easily understood. "Words cannot capture it," Suzuki says, which seemed to me like clever rationalization. The undisclosed secret is more like the deception behind the magician's trick. Until you have joined the union, so to speak, the trick is not revealed, and when you are party to the trick, you must swear to keep the secret.

I tried to empty my mind and contemplate the sound of one hand clapping, as I was told it is possible to do. I could not. I tried to picture my original face before my parents were born. I could not. I asked myself how it might have been possible for an adolescent girl or a peasant with minimal education to solve the riddle, as is alleged, when I couldn't. If they could succeed, surely I should be able to, I reasoned. And then, I did, and found to my great delight, that it was not rocket science, after all.

Simply put, the mind must be stilled in order for the body to do well, and performing with a mind that is so focused on the act, that it is otherwise a blank, is Zen.

That is all there is to it! But, a stilled and emptied mind is not easy to achieve, because a conscious effort to make the mind a blank uses the mind. This paradox cannot be easily explained in words but can be suggested by action.

The following examples demonstrate this philosophy.

When Hyakujo, the Zen master was searching for his replacement he created a contest. He placed a vase of water on the ground and asked: "Who can say what this is without naming it?" The chief monk contemplated the question at length and secretly posted his answer: "No one can call it a geta (wooden shoe)." A minor monk kicked over the vase and left. Hyakujo made the minor monk the next Zen master.

Does this story or the winning response make any sense? Bizarre – would be the normal western reaction.

When Zen says subject and object are one and indivisible, the dualistic western mind finds the statement incomprehensible. How can I (subject) and you (object) be one and the same? When we rephrase the statement, though, and say the person (subject) and his behavior (object) are one and the same, the statement becomes more acceptable. It becomes clearer still when we say "what is" and "what we think it is" are one and the same – mind and matter are one. Thus a vase is a vase is a vase. It cannot be defined by what it is not because that answer is caught up in the duality of what it is and what we think it is; distinctions of a readily deceived mind . Better to knock it over!

Let me cite another story. The Zen master instructs his pupil: "Take this stick and kill the snake." The student thrashes about with the stick. The master takes away the stick and breaks it in two. "There," he says, "the snake is dead." That is to say "the snake is the stick and the stick is the snake."

These anecdotes are teasing and tantalizing. I get it. I understand. It's all very clear, it seems – and then, the clarity evaporates, like the daylight that hides behind a dark cloud.

There is a calmness that comes when we achieve physical peace; that is, when we can perform an act without a preoccupation of success or failure. And there is even more calmness when we achieve mental peace; that is, when there are no wandering thoughts. Finally, if we achieve value peace; that is, when we can behave compassionately with no wandering desires, we have captured the total essence of Zen.

The traditional method used to encourage enlightenment consists of stylistic meditation whereby the subject sits on a cushion facing a blank wall. This is called zazen. The physical posture is important. The legs must be crossed with the soles upward upon the thighs. This is the full lotus position and can only be achieved with long practice. The hands rest on the lap left over right, the palms upward and the thumbs touching each other. The body is held erect. The eyes are open and gaze at a point on the floor a few feet ahead. Breathing is slow, originating from the abdomen, with concentration on the expiration. At the beginning, the breathing is counted to ten, repeatedly. The Vietnamese Zen monk, Thich Nhat Hanh, admonishes: breathe in, breathe out, pause, smile; for a genuine smile can come only from an awakened mind.

The center of the sentient being lies at the pit of the stomach according to Buddhism. Anybody with a western education will find this claim difficult to comprehend. The headquarters for our thinking selves is in the brain. That's where thinking occurs! That's where the neurons are! How can the center of our being be lower down, at the base of our tummy, no less? It seems totally unreasonable. But then, I contemplated the truly emotional events in my life; the time I almost had a serious automobile accident, sliding towards an oncoming bus on a slippery slope; the time I mislaid all my identification papers abroad; the time a girl I fancied said she had gotten engaged; the time my good friend told me my father had inoperable stomach cancer. I did not feel the impact in my head. I felt it in the pit of my stomach. The brain may lie within the skull but the soul may well be located outside the head. Why not in the pit of the abdomen?

If you want to climb a mountain, begin at the top, a Zen master says. Is it nonsense? Not really, I take it to mean you should visualize the conquest before you begin the climb. Mahatma Gandhi, the Hindu reformer, made a similar claim: "If you want to be somewhere, be there."

Consider how anyone learns to walk, swim, ride a bike, or play tennis. He stumbles, falters, and he falls, but as he keeps practicing, he begins to succeed and eventually, he can carry out these tasks without a conscious effort. The same principle could apply as well to more difficult tasks, like playing the piano or performing surgery. Practice and practice until the performance becomes effortless. The mind must be freed from the preoccupation of success or failure. There should be no thought of whether you can do it. That is a given! The most demanding task must elicit no nervous twitch, no nervous sweat.

I do that now when I am in the operating room — calm, cool, and collected. I wish I had known about this when I was ten years old because I would not have lost my judo match.

A number of books have been written on "Zen and the Art of ..." Robert Pirsig's "Zen and the Art of Motorcycle Maintenance" being the most widely acclaimed. I have recently reread the book and found certain passages more riveting than when I first read it. I'm glad I used the word "gumption" to describe Japanese-Canadians who resisted government coercion. Persig, I suspect, would have approved. In the Zen book on tennis called "The Inner Game of Tennis" Timothy Gallwey talks about how to beat your opponent in a friendly game. When you're at the net you say: "What happened to your backhand, you couldn't do that before." Your opponent will become so preoccupied with what he is doing differently his game will fall apart. This trick is probably too well known to work today. Certainly the admonition to call out "bounce, hit; bounce, hit" works, because the mind does not have time to become preoccupied with interfering thoughts.

Practice long and hard, then perform with a mind freed from all preoccupations, seems like a good motto for surgeons-in-training, but imagine suggesting that every surgery program in the country should strive to produce a Zen surgeon.

Narrow minded "Christians" will be up in arms. "We are a Christian institution!" they will cry. "Why should we support an institution that will not uphold our religious values?"

We do confuse religion and philosophy. When Christ admonished his followers to turn the other cheek, did He mean that only those who were His followers should do so?

I discussed my understanding of Zen with Dr. G. Victor Sogen Hori, of the Faculty of Religious Studies at McGill, and for nine years, a Zen monk, in Japan. He has written about his experiences, how learning occurs in a Zen monastery and his views about the Zen koan. He has experienced his personal awakening and solved his koans. He could have stayed in Japan, as a roshi or Zen master but he elected to return to Canada to an academic appointment at McGill. Perhaps when I study his book, "Zen Sand: the book of Capping Phrases for Koan Practice," I will achieve a deeper under-standing of Zen. Already I have acquired a new appreciation of the Zen koan. Dr. Hori argues that the koan originated from the Chinese literary culture – its competitiveness, its deception, the spontaneity, the turning of the table, the mind-to-mind transmission that is not founded on words or letters, are all part of that tradition. Dr. Hori's book is about Zen "capping phrases." These are concise prepared statements which, when memorized, provide the appropriate repartee for an assigned koan. The roshi provides the koan and the student, by his "capping phrase" denotes whether or not he has solved his koan. Dr. Hori undertook to compile and translate about four thousand of these phrases which are rendered in three languages: Japanese, Chinese, and English – no small accomplishment! Furthermore, Dr. Hori disagrees with the idea that Zen cannot be captured in words. "Zen does not reject language," he says, "but is freed in language by mastering it." It is altogether a delightful concept.

Dr. Hori was gracious in not being very critical of my remarks but he said my grasp of Zen was rather shallow. Furthermore, he reprimanded me for not emphasizing a moral dimension to any action. According to my description, he said, a person could commit a robbery, or murder, for that matter, and be so focused on the act, I would qualify it as Zen behavior.

Was my understanding of Zen so superficial as to make it meaningless? Perhaps; but then, perhaps not. I thought about my grasp of Zen and compared it to my knowledge of Christianity. I imagined a few dialogues.

"Life is suffering," says a Buddhist.

"No, life is sin," says the Christian.

"The suffering is due to desire," says the Buddhist. "Take away the desire and you eliminate the suffering."

"Repent your sin," says the Christian. "Believe in Christ and you will find everlasting life."

"The formula for a life devoid of unhealthy cravings consists of following the eight-fold paths," says the Buddhist. The right aspiration, the right effort, the right concentration, the right understanding (the Four Noble Truths), the right mindfulness, the right action, the right livelihood and the right speech. I even created an acronym so I could remember them – *m. a. u. l. s. e. a.* creatures.

These eight-fold paths had a familiar ring – as if I had heard of them before. I was at a Buddhist service just once in my life, and that, as a child. I couldn't have heard about them from my school-teachers because I don't think they were Buddhists, nor from my friends, nor even from the church ministers. And then it struck me. I had heard them from my own parents.

"Grow up and become somebody worthy of respect, worthy of honor," my mother would often say. "Study hard, and always do the right thing!" My mother became a devout Christian, but I suspect that in some ways, she reverted to her Buddhist roots in raising her children.

Another dialogue.

"If I rob a bank and kill a teller in the process, but I repent my sin, will all be forgiven? Will I escape confinement in a penitentiary?" the Buddhist asks.

"No, but you will find more peace by confessing to the crime than by not confessing. Your soul may be saved although you may rot in prison," says the Christian.

"That is important, is it?" asks the Buddhist.

"Yes," says the Christian.

"I don't get it," says the Buddhist.

"You would if you had a deeper knowledge of Christianity," says the Christian.

And, finally, another dialogue; this with a putative Zen master.

"An understanding of Zen came to you in a flash. What, then, is the sound of one hand clapping?"

"Thunder, after a distant flash of lightening," I reply.

"Explain it!"

"All right. Imagine the sound of many hands clapping. Thundering applause, deafening noise. Now, imagine someone totally focused on some act, so free of preoccupations, everything else is blanked out. The sound of many hands clapping is a deathly silence to him. And, if you can imagine that, the corollary must also be true; the sound of no-noise can be as loud as anything you can imagine. Thunder and lightening is a particularly apt metaphor, I think, because the thunder may be heard long after the flash of lightening. We know why that is so. Sound travels at a fraction of the speed of light, but this reality is strange to our perception. We see the lightening bolt, why should there be a delay before we hear the sound. The question of the sound of one hand clapping addresses this question of perception and reality in my estimation: perception may suggest a duality; reality is non-duality, the lightening and the thunder are one."

"Is that the correct answer to this koan?"

"I don't know. It is as far as I am concerned."

Zen views the basic nature of man as perfection itself. Our ability to think and to remember, though, distorts the mind and creates delusions. We are forever mistaking delusions for reality. Eliminate all delusions and discover enlightenment, or awakening, it says.

I suppose it's all right to speculate about these things although, to me, it's like arguing about the number of angels that can dance on the head of a pin — largely irrelevant!

I had another meeting with Dr. Hori.

"What is the moral dimension of Zen?" I asked.

"Compassion," he replied, without a moment's hesitation.

"Of course!" I thought, "Why had it not occurred to me earlier?" This was, after all, familiar territory. As a doctor I know that compassion is more important than any other emotion. Compassion is different from sympathy, which can suggest condescension, a sense of pity, and is different from empathy which implies an intellectual awareness but not, necessarily, a genuine concern. Compassion has no sense of superiority, it is simply being in tune with another's emotions. Zen is entirely compassionate; therefore, compassion is fundamental to Zen.

Must a Zen surgeon spend a period of preparation in a Zen monastery, just as a medical doctor would have had to attend and graduate from a school of Medicine, or a lawyer from a Law School? Can I claim to be a Zen surgeon without this experience? A Zen surgeon would be guided by the eightfold paths. He would be compassionate and, at the same time, he would be so focused on the task at hand that everything else would be blanked out of his mind. I do not think it is wrong for me to aspire to these goals any more than it would be wrong for any doctor to try to be a "Christian" surgeon without ever having been baptized.

I recall a patient who came to me once with a nasty complication following a routine operation. The doctor who had performed the surgery had told the patient he had done the procedure so many times he could do it now with his eyes closed. "... and the bastard did it with his eyes closed," the patient complained to me. It was not a Zen performance. I remember, as well, a funeral director who needed an operation to correct a problem in his kidney. "Do a good job, Doc," he said to me as he was being wheeled into the operating room, "all I see are the mistakes!"

The Zen Surgeon

I will describe two surgical procedures as they might be performed by a Zen surgeon. (I do this because it is important that you understand the simplicity and the complexity of the two tasks.) The first, a vasectomy, is a simple, ten minute, outpatient procedure performed under a local anaesthetic and the second, a radical prostatectomy, is major cancer surgery. I estimate that I may have carried out ten thousand vasectomies and, perhaps, a thousand radical prostatectomies. (I have described details on how I do these operations in previous publications; vasectomy in a book called *Private Parts*, and radical prostatectomy in a book called *The Prostate: Everything you need to know about the Man Gland.*)

The challenge with a vasectomy is not in the numbers, of course, but in how often it can be done with minimal disturbance to the patient. The candidate, after all, is awake and is quite aware of every discomfort, including the pain of a needle prick that is used to freeze the skin. Patients vary in their level of anxiety as they climb aboard the operating table. Some men are so agitated they cannot lie still. They wriggle and squirm with the application of a skin cleansing solution to disinfect the scrotal skin, and the odd one bolts upright and literally jumps off the table. A handful of patients have actually declined the procedure at this point. The vast majority of men grit their teeth, lie quietly, and I become aware of how nervous they were only at the end of the procedure when I see a pool of perspiration on the paper sheet covering the table.

The vas deferens is a long, thick walled, small-caliber tube about two or three millimetres in diameter, which runs a course from the bottom of the testicle to the groin and then into the back of the prostate. When I pinch the structure within the scrotum between my thumb and index finger the tube lies inertly, like a rope, in a relaxed patient but, in the nervous candidate, the vas is lively and wiggles, like a snake. This apparent "wriggling" of the vas occurs because the patient unintentionally contracts the dartos muscle which lies under the skin of the scrotum. Normally, the dartos muscle contracts in the cold to bring the testicle closer to the body to warm it up, and relaxes in the heat to keep the testicles four degrees cooler than the rest of the body. I am amazed at the power of these muscular contractions. It reminds me of landing a fish already hooked. How can a fish so small produce so much pull? The needle I use to freeze the skin is very thin, a gauge twenty-nine, thinner even than those used for an insulin injection or for an immunization, and the insertion can be made almost painless if the stab is quick and the instillation is slow. A Zen surgeon will allay the fears and concerns of his patient, cajoling him with distracting conversation, comforting him with encouragement. Even for such a minor procedure, there must be the right effort, the right mindfulness on the part of the surgeon. I do this with a silent challenge to myself. Can I perform the procedure painlessly and without losing a drop of blood? I often succeed, but not always. And when I don't succeed, the challenge is still to remain focused and to do the right thing. Very often, I feel I am a Zen surgeon at work when I do a vasectomy. Once in a while, though, I lose more than a few drops of blood and I have to resort to more burning with the electro-cautery. At that point, I am at risk of no longer being a Zen surgeon.

A radical retropubic prostatectomy, on the other hand, is performed in the operating room of a hospital under a full anaesthetic or the area under attack completely frozen. Often, the anaesthesiologist will administer an epidural along with the general, place a central line (a needle into the neck vein to monitor blood volume), and a needle into the wrist artery (radial) to measure oxygen levels in the blood. The usual case may take up to two or two and a half hours and the blood loss can be as much as a liter; thus, it is no minor undertaking. When the diagnosis is early and the patient otherwise healthy, I expect a life-long cure with complete recovery of urine control as well as a full recovery of functional erections.

How does a Zen surgeon achieve this? He will be guided by the eight-fold paths and be ever vigilant while transfixed on the task at hand. He will carry out the steps of the procedure with the facility that comes from long practice. He will not be rattled because his mind will not wander. The different steps of the procedure are like putting together a new electrical appliance or a child's toy that requires assembly. Ignore the instructions at your peril. Do the steps out of turn and there is going to be a price to be paid, a hitch, a need to redo a step, an unnecessary complication. Steps for a radical retropubic prostatectomy are meaningful only to urologic surgeons but I will describe them here just to provide a sense of what needs to be done.

Make a four inch midline vertical incision below the umbilicus and above the pubic bone. Open the rectus sheath in the midline and spread apart the recti muscles to be held laterally by a self retaining retractor fixed to the operating table. Incise the endopelvic fascia, bunch and ligate the veins over the bladder neck and prostate, free the pubo-prostatic ligaments, control the dorsal vein complex with a suture ligature, delineate the urethro-prostatic junction, open the anterior urethra, place the two anterior anastomotic stitches inside-out at the two and ten o'clock positions, transsect the urethra, free the posterior and lateral attachments and fold back the prostate, cut DeNonvillier's fascia, free up the seminal vesicles and the ampulla of the vas deferens, dissect the prostate off the bladder neck, evert the lining of the bladder neck, place the two posterior anastomotic stitches into the urethra at the four and eight o'clock position, and fix them to the posterior aspect of the bladder neck, insert the catheter, place the anterior stitches to the bladder neck, tie the four anastomotic stitches, place a drain, and close the wound. The steps are always the same, but differences in human anatomy, distribution of the blood vessels, fat deposits, and elasticity of tissue are amazingly varied. During one operation, I said to my resident: "You're sweating like a stuffed pig, and I'm not perspiring at all. I must get you to study Zen." An unfair, even demeaning statement, perhaps, but meant, nonetheless, to drive that student to reflect upon his current condition. Had I felt that this resident would be crushed by my remark, I would not have made it. Some residents are thin-skinned, and others are not. My role is to adjust my remarks according to the resident.

I didn't think it was possible to become skilled in Zen without a stint in the monastery until I re-read Alan Watts' book *The Way of Zen,* perhaps the most readable vernacular account. Historically, according to Watts, awakening came to devotees, *before* formal meditation (zazen) and koans became part of the curriculum. Solving the koans and prolonged meditations were adopted, according to Watts, to cope with the enormous popularity of Zen and the inability of the limited numbers of masters to cope with the demand. Of course a person could not become a Zen master, or roshi, without formal preparation, but Zen principles can be a part of any line of work, including surgery. At least, that is what I believe. Awakening is said to have come to a illiterate Chinese peasant when he was just a boy. Hui-neng (637-713) eventually became a Zen master with a large following, but his original enlightenment occurred without benefit of koans or stylized meditations; all this to say that I believe that the study... perhaps the mastery of Zen is achievable by anyone who truly desires it.

I suspect that some devotees may quarrel with my sounding off on Zen. "Those who speak do not know, those who know do not speak," they will say, repeating the lines attributed to Tai Te Ching. Am I not like a charlatan passing out medical advice without attending medical school, a masquerading Zen surgeon? Perhaps so, but I would argue that not all medical advice from doctors is good, nor from laymen, bad. In fact, some doctors give very bad advice. Doctors who argue against diagnostic tests that can lead to earlier diagnosis of cancer, like the rectal exam and the serial PSA blood tests for the prostate and the mammogram for the breast, don't make sense to me.

But how should a Zen surgeon behave when he is out of the operating theater? It is one thing to strive for extraordinary focus in the operating room, but a surgeon does not spend all his time performing surgery. Do Zen principles apply to office practice? Must a Zen surgeon spend designated periods of the day in meditation, in the lotus position, in long robes?

I argue that the long years of surgical training are like the period of training in a Zen monastery. The average training period for a surgeon, after high school, is fifteen years. There are four years of undergraduate university studies, four years of medical school, five years of specialty training and two years of Fellowship training. Interestingly, fifteen years is usually the time taken by a monk in Zen training to become a master. The surgeon-in-training must learn how to cope with the inhumane hours and the impossible demands of his workload. He learns the trade largely by watching, imitating, and doing, just as the monks-in-training learn their trade. One day, the monk is working the garden, the next day, he must prepare the evening meal for the entire assembly. In anticipation of that new chore, each monk-in-training pays close attention to what the senior monks are doing, learning by watching and imitating. When the monks are sent out to beg for food, the task is not unlike that of a resident who must learn to cope with the hierarchy of power and learn how to fit in without ruffling feathers.

I believe Zen principles can be applied to everyday living and can be considered by anyone in any walk of life. It should not be privy only to those who have taken up residence in a Zen monastery. In fact, Zen principles are part of everyday life. A store clerk announces over the loudspeaker that an item in column six is now on sale. There is no nervousness in her voice, the statement is made clearly and confidently. If this same clerk is handed a microphone and asked to make a speech in front of an audience, she freezes, stammers, and becomes incoherent. We might see the same thing with a train conductor who confidently announces the next train stop, but ask him to comment on gay marriages and he may become totally inarticulate. Why does this happen? It is the overactive mind that interferes with the performance. How foolish will I appear? Will my pounding heart be picked up by the microphone? Will I stutter and stammer? We are our own worst enemy. As Pogo has said: "We have seen the enemy, and he is us".

There are Zen books on archery, sword-fighting, and even the tea ceremony. And there are professionals whose writings reflect an appre-ciation of Zen. I am thinking of psychiatrists, like Carl Jung and Erich Fromm, poets like Walt Whitman, writers and philosophers, like Antoine de Saint-Exupery and Henry David Thoreau. I believe that people, like Alan Watts, who popu-larized Zen without committing to it, should not be denigrated because he chose to remain at a lower level than that of a "roshi". I applaud Dr. Hori for returning to North America rather than remaining a roshi in Japan. He has taken on, in my view, a greater challenge.

My Zen challenge in every day life is to strive to be compassionate no matter what the circumstances and regardless of reward; to practice my profession with such intensity, with such focus, that I will have nothing else on my mind.

Ironies

If paradox, an absurd statement that expresses a possible truth, is the stuff of Zen, ironies are the stuff of life. I have had my share of them.

Place

Waking up in the room in which I was born (October 1982)

It was an October morning in 1982, after my first night in Japan after an absence of forty-five years, and my mother asked:

"Yoku neta ka? (Did you sleep well?)

"Hai, yoku nemashita"(Yes, very well), I responded.

"Yokaata," (That's good) she said, "soko de umaleta no yo" (That's the room you were born in.) It boggled my mind.

Time

In 1988 I was in Vancouver promoting my book *"Private Parts"*. Between radio, television, and newspaper appearances, there was some unscheduled time and I was asked what I wanted to see or do. I asked to be taken to Hasting's Park. The young lady assigned to look after me seemed puzzled by my request but made her inquiries. "Oh," she said, after she had done her homework, " you want to go to the old Exhibition grounds." When we got there, the hilly terrain rang faint bells and the animal quarters looked strangely familiar, I walked up to the barn door and peered in. The long pipe struts supporting the roof were there as I had remembered them, but what was most striking was the strong stench of the animals, as the horses and cows were back in their stalls.

Outside the barn door there was a pristine yellow plaque, commemorating the internment of the Japanese-Canadians. I felt my eyes watering, as I saw this understated, simple reminder of such a horrific action.

Age

The army officer in command of the Farnham camp, where captured German officers had been detained and where we were sent after the war, was a fellow named Oscar Beaudet. He was a military man and ruled the camp with an iron fist, commanding attention because of his loud and trained military voice. He was an imposing figure I dared not cross.

Decades later, Oscar became my patient. I operated on his enlarged prostate gland that had caused a urinary retention. Far from the intimidating figure I remembered from years past, he was now a senile, shriveled up elderly man. "How the mighty have fallen," I thought. He said he remembered me, or rather, remembered my father. "A good man," he said. His daughter was going to pass over his archives to me, but somehow we got our signals crossed and I never did receive them.

Competency

Soon after I began my practice my colleagues at the hospital invited me to join them in a group clinical practice that was being formed. But, as I was actively involved in research at the time, and as that activity generated no income, I was asked to accept a lesser slice of the earnings pie.

"What you are suggesting," I said, "is that I am equally competent during the off hours and on week-ends, but less so during the work week. I must respectfully decline to join your partnership." And I didn't.

Years later, when I was one of the busier practitioners, with a new regime in place, a partnership practice was proposed with all partners largely homogenized regardless of their contribution to the pool. There was no monetary incentive to work as hard, but there would be less quibbling over access to operating time or to bed allocation. The scheme was communism in its purest form.

Our group practice worked for years. We added refinements. A small percentage of our clinical earnings was kept apart, and redistributed according to merit in teaching, research, administration, and clinical work, as judged by a small in-house committee. The difference between the largest "bonus" and the smallest was minuscule, but has remained a bone of contention every year.

Our chief (Mostafa Elhilila) who conceived and implemented the plan has been widely acclaimed, and our practice plan has been paraded as a model within the university community; however, some of the very people who supported the scheme now wish to abandon it. "Communism has never worked," they argue. "A new chief cannot be recruited," another argument goes, "without a two-tiered system – one inflated income for the chief, and another for the rest of the staff." But, the workers have protested. "Why should it be necessary to abandon a scheme that is the envy of the institution?" I am somewhat bemused by it all, but I feel privileged to have participated in a social experiment that actually worked.

Actually, the scheme was not so unique. Japanese companies practiced it. Once an employee was hired, he was hired for life. If he turned out to be a lazy or incompetent worker, he was not dismissed. The others simply took up the slack and pitied the worker who could not be more productive. To give further evidence of the power of this philosophy, let me recall the time when a major earthquake hit Kobe and severely damaged Japan's largest steel mill. The other steel companies took over the orders, but passed over the profits of those transactions so that the Kobe plant could be rebuilt.

It is interesting to muse upon the fact that the ironies of my life have been, in effect, the truths of it. From the moment of conception until the present day, place, time, age and competency have been the forces which have controlled my career, and I have been able to control only one of them; that of competency.

On Learning and Teaching

When I was five years old, I was sent to a Japanese language kindergarten, and then to an English language public school the year after. I could not speak nor understand a word of English and, from the beginning, school assignments were onerous challenges for me. My first language was Japanese, so I had difficulty with the pronunciation of certain words. "Red" came out as "led" and "rice" as "lice" no matter how hard I tried to get the pronunciation right. We always spoke Japanese at home, and my parents expected the school to teach me the "foreign tongue." I was born left-handed but I was forced to use my right hand as was customary at the time. This was achieved by strapping a bell, like the ones placed on a kitten's collar, to the wrist of my left hand. Whenever I used a crayon or a pencil with this hand, the bell would tingle and alert the teacher. She would come by and tap the back of my left hand with a long ruler to remind me of the error of my ways. Today I am grateful I write with my right hand, but I still paint with my left and I am a left-handed surgeon.

I was slow to read. Whenever it was my turn in class, I would stumble and falter, and my comprehension of what I had read would disappear. In retrospect, I think I suffered from a form of dyslexia, which I managed to resolve on my own. The trick was to focus on a spot ahead of the word I was supposed to read.

I remember my first years in school as a horrific experience. I detested every moment, and the fact that I was promoted repeatedly did little to assuage the discomfort and insecurity, which filled my every day.

I suffered from bed-wetting long after most boys were dry. I don't know if the two, language problems and bed-wetting, are connected in some manner or not, but it is interesting to posit whether bed-wetting had anything to do with my choice of Urology as a career.

At the end of my third academic year, the Stanford-Binet IQ test was administered at the war camp. I scored so badly, I was asked to repeat the year. This did not bother me much, but it did upset my parents. They seemed so devastated that I resolved never to disappoint them again with a poor academic performance. I don't believe I ever fumbled another test. I might have come close with the spot anatomy quiz in first-year medicine, which is an interesting challenge in itself. There are several stations set up in the anatomy lab, and each student is given only twenty seconds to solve the "puzzle of the station". A typical experience would be the sight of an arm bone, with a red dot painted on it. The typewritten question would be "What is the name of the muscle which inserts here?" By the time you figured out that it was indeed an arm bone, it would be time to move on to the next station. Later, I found out that the students who scored well on these tests had access to a bank of questions from previous years. They had been coached for a grade instead of for the knowledge the grade was supposed to represent. There is much too much of this even at the university level. When I was an eighth grader in a public school in Montreal, the class sat the Stanford-Binet, or its equivalent. I managed to learn my score. It was 127! What was my IQ score when I had been asked to repeat the year? How relevant are the numbers when English is not your first language? If an IQ can change to an acceptable level in a few years, how reflective is it of native intelligence? How can you compare two people of the same age when one has been exposed to a new language for a fraction of the time of the other? I am convinced IQ quotients reflect social integration and I remain reluctant to this day to accept test scores of any kind as important determinants. Years later, when I was the Program Director of Urology at McGill, I was responsible for selecting the candidates for training. My one regret was in being outvoted one year, when I preferred an applicant who had come to Canada as a boat-person from Viet Nam. His marks were mediocre, but his dossier indicated that, while a medical student, he held two jobs, one at MacDonald's, while he learned English, his third language.

During our first year in Montreal, I was enrolled in a local public school called Peace Centennial. My teacher's name was Mrs. Trueman. I never got to know her first name but I wondered if she had any connection with Harry S. Truman, the US president, despite the difference in spelling. I didn't know how to bring up the subject and couldn't think of how I could ever do so. The question I wanted to ask her was whether president Truman would have agreed to drop an atomic bomb on an occidental city. This may seem extraordinarily astute for a thirteen year old, so it is possible that I was merely repeating a question asked by my elders; however, the devastating effect of the atomic bomb weighed heavily on my mind. I was conscious, as well, that there were two classes of Canadians, and that I was not a member of the first. The schoolwork itself was not difficult; the camp schools had prepared me well. The only new subject was French which my classmates had started in the third grade, thus making it necessary for me to play 'catch-up' for the four years I had missed. Thankfully, this was not difficult, and I was able to follow the group in a surprisingly short period. My English-speaking classmates knew very little French and saw no point in learning more. "The French should learn English!" was their attitude.

What was strikingly different from the schools in the war camps was the gymnasium. There were ropes to climb, assortments of balls, and mats to tumble upon. I had no idea how I stood academically but I knew I excelled in art. Mrs. Trueman entered me in a province-wide competition and my entry won. I was awarded a scholarship to an art school run by Arthur Lismer of the Group of Seven. I remained a student there throughout my years in high school and I attended classes there even when I was in university, because the museum school continued to maintain me as a scholarship student. I learned how to use charcoal, how to sketch a nude, how to create a design, and how to paint and sculpt. My favorite art form was sculpture, however, and my interest was focused on the molding of human forms. I must admit that one of the more difficult decisions I had to make in life was whether to pursue a career in art or to become a doctor. Mr. Lismer was fond of me, I think, because he was also left handed. He often doodled at my easel, and I remember being upset that my artwork was being ruined. If I had kept his renditions, as I could have, I would now own original artwork done by a master, and worth a small fortune.

The realization that I could compete with the best of my class-mates occurred to me when I was in grade eight, the first year of high school. One day, I was caught kibitzing during a math class. The teacher was furious. When I protested that I had finished the assignment the teacher, Miss Hamilton, demanded that I come up to her desk and show it to her. The look of utter astonishment on her face when she saw that I had indeed completed the work is etched in my memory. I also found that visualizing an object from another viewpoint, the basic objective of a subject called mechanical drawing, came easily to me. Perhaps this reinforced the possibility of becoming a surgeon in later years.

The following year I was elected class president, a position that brought with it, some interesting problems. One day, a student brought in a deck of cards with photographs of nude women in lewd poses on its back. Everybody sneaked a look. The student had "borrowed" it from his older brother who had purchased it in New York City. One class-mate was outraged. He took the deck and trashed it. Because I was the class president, the matter was brought for me to arbitrate. I listened as my friends made their pleas. Could I imagine the trouble that awaited my class-mate who "borrowed" the deck? He didn't have permission in the first place, so his big brother was going to beat the living daylights out of him. The other class-mate was unmoved; his moral indignation, sincere and genuine; in fact, he thought he should be commended for his action. I wisely decided this was not a problem where I could turn to the teacher for help, and so I proposed the following solution. "As the deck of cards had been taken without permission, it must be returned," I said. "And, as every class-mate had taken a peek we must all contribute toward the purchase of a replacement." Solomon's decision, I thought at the time; a kind of cop-out if you were to ask me today. I make mention of this small event, only because I am now called upon to make life-and-death decisions; a far cry from the then-important playing card arbitrations. Life has its way of teaching you the meaning of priorities.

In our second year of high school, we were asked what we planned to do with our lives; to what occupation we aspired. To help us with our decision, a vocational guidance test was administered and, at its conclusion, there was the customary query: Do you have any questions? I wrote down: "Is it true that if you are a Japanese-Canadian, you cannot practice law or architecture?" This led to a summons to appear before the principal.

"Where did you get such a notion?" the principal asked. "We live in a democracy where that kind of thing is just not tolerated."

But, it turned out that I was right. A Japanese-Canadian could study law or architecture, all right, but he might not be licenced to practice it. He could, however, study medicine, and become a practicing physician.

My final two years of high school, now at the High School of Montreal, across the street from McGill university, reinforced my intention to pursue Medicine as a career. Some of my class-mates in the new school were Jewish, and becoming a medical student was an ultimate goal sought by many of them. It was rumored that no matter how outstanding their qualifications, just a dozen or so Jewish students would be admitted to McGill's medical school each year. If there was an oriental quota at the time, I was unaware of it; nonetheless, I chose Latin over geography at the beginning of high school with the mistaken notion that the dead language was an absolute prerequisite.

On a more lively note, my occidental classmates in high school and my Japanese-Canadian friends in the community were now exploring the wonders of the opposite sex. I was no different and I was attracted to every pretty girl I encountered. Two things saved me from becoming sidetracked and from an impending disaster. First, I was covered with zits and was ugly, as the mirror constantly reminded me. Secondly, I fervently wanted to study medicine and I was not going to be readily distracted from that goal. My art lessons and paper route provided reasons to excuse myself from social engagements. Had I been handsome and attractive to girls though, I suspect I would not have been able to resist overtures that might have come in my direction. Fortunately, I was able to concentrate on my studies. I spent long hours at my desk, largely in day-dreams, as my studies were far from focused. Nevertheless, my marks were in the eighties and nineties when the high school matriculation results were announced.

My poorest score was in English composition. My efforts always earned the comments "good imagination" but I never learned proper conjugation and accurate punctuation. I suspect I was supposed to have learned that during the war years.

My second poorest mark was in French. The French lessons at the junior high school I attended, were often ludicrous. Sometimes they consisted of instructions to open the text to a certain page and to start reading. Of course we did everything but follow the order. The teacher, in the meantime, busied herself with the English-language morning newspaper. Although I realize that this is far from a stunning accolade for this particular teacher, it nonetheless helps to explain my lack of motivation to learn this rich language.

In those days (1951) we progressed from high school to university with no junior college as a prerequisite. I was ready. University fees were not exorbitant and were independent, I discovered, of the number of courses taken. I did not have the marks to be awarded a scholarship, especially with my mediocre grades in English and French, but I applied for and was awarded a bursary. The B.A. student took four courses and the B.Sc. student took five. I registered for six. The extra subject was Greek Philosophy, a course taken by only a handful of students. I was fascinated with the Greek philosophers who pondered, long before the time of Christ, the basis of all things. This search for order continues to this day with physicists contemplating a unified theory: one hypothesis to explain all the laws of nature. This intense curiosity about order, about a plausible explanation of natural laws would serve me well, later, in my medical career.

In the second year, I took the introductory courses in Psychology, organic chemistry and comparative zoology; all deemed pre-requisites for Medicine. Professor Donald Hebb taught the

Psychology course. He lectured to an amorphous class of hundreds of students from a microphone at a podium at the head of a large auditorium. Once, to prove that hypnotism was merely the power of suggestion, he proposed to put the class to sleep; at least all those who wished to participate; while the others could remain spectators. I felt myself falling under his spell, but decided to be an observer. The power of suggestion was awesome.

Years later, when I was a resident doctor, I claimed I could hypnotize willing volunteers at a party. Several nurses dared me, so I did. When the three volunteers slumped over in a deep sleep, I panicked and immediately asked them to open their eyes, realizing that a little power in untrained hands could be a very dangerous combination.

I have, though, used the power of suggestion in practice. A woman had to have her kidney removed but was terrified of post-operative pain. I told her that should she suffer inordinate pain, I would press a site near the incision and her pain would dissipate. Fortunately for her and for me, it worked just as I had surmised.

When the marks for all the courses were posted at the end of the academic year, I was surprised to find my name third from the top in Psychology, behind two senior students. At that point, I decided to apply for entry into the Honours program in Psychology for the final two years. I felt it was my key to an acceptance into the medical faculty, and I was right.

I was beginning to appreciate the next-to-impossible goal I had set for myself in pursuing Medicine as a career. I read the ten best novels ever written and then expanded the list to twenty. I read biographies of famous people, and I read Time magazine regularly to prepare myself for the medical aptitude test all applicants were required to take. In my readings, I discovered that Albert Einstein saw little merit in shaving cream; he thought soap and water worked just as well so I adopted his frugal habit. I learned that, in his youth, Thomas Edison had a fat friend who was poorly coordinated and hopeless at sports but he could throw his spit further than anybody else. Edison wondered why throwing spit should not be considered as important as hitting a baseball or throwing a football. Interesting point, I thought. Perhaps, if all the vectors for good and bad were added up, all people were equal. It was a mind-set that gave me a lot of self confidence. Fyodor Dostoevsky, I decided, was the world's best novelist, "*Crime and Punishment*" the best novel ever written. "*Moby Dick*", in my view, the most overrated. Bertrand Russell, I concluded, was the most palatable philosopher, and philosophical issues the most fascinating. I remain a voracious reader, a bibliophile, and I am most entertained by novelists who take liberties with actual history – like James Clavell, Nikos Kazantzakis, and, more recently, Dan Brown and Philip Roth. I prefer clever plotting to skillful writing.

I was comfortable with my preparation and I thought I was ready for the MCAT (Medical College Aptitude Test). I had no idea, at the time, that I was competing with applicants from privileged backgrounds; sons and daughters of university professors, and boys and girls who were products of private schools and personal tutoring.

I was totally backward, at the same time, in the social graces. I had my hair cut at home and I was raised to buy a second shoe when the old one was beyond repair. It was fortunate for me that sartorial statements were not part of the application process. The social graces, I later discovered, were very easily acquired. The officers' mess hall, for example, was where I learned dining etiquette; that all-too-formalized rituals of eating with the right utensil at the appropriate time, and drinking from the correct glass. These choreographed behaviours, like the Japanese tea ceremony, do not impress me. They emphasize irrelevant matters, as far as I am concerned.

The tiny note on a piece of paper five-by-seven inches which signaled my acceptance into the medical faculty may have been another ritualized act, but it was a Godsend. I was elated! I immediately set out to seek advice as to how to make sure I would not flunk out. I had doctor relatives in Japan, my mother told me, but they were of no use to me. I sought out Japanese-Canadians who had become doctors or who were in the process of becoming doctors. Soi Isomura had just graduated and was most helpful. Community gossip had it that he was a brilliant student in theoretical physics but when he learned that men, like J. Robert Oppenheimer were questioning the morality of nuclear physics, he decided to abandon the field and switch to medicine. He gave me a number of his textbooks.

Jim Hasegawa was a year ahead of me in dental school. He let me see his notes in Histology, a course taken by both medical and dental students. His writing was so legible, and his illustrations so well done, that I wondered how I could ever succeed. Jim was a gold medallist when he graduated and has had a successful dental career in Montreal. I had known of Jim, "Shiro", as he was known then, since the year I spent in New Denver. He had lived in an adjacent war camp, called Roseberry, four miles from New Denver, and he ran the distance daily as a high school student. He studied at Sir George Williams College, now Concordia University, at night; all the while, holding down a full-time job during the day, and he eventually went to McGill, in order to complete his Dentistry degree. Today, Concordia excels in graduating students in fine arts and computer science among other disciplines, and its rector Dr. Frederick Lowy is my close friend and class-mate from Psychology and Medical School days.

When the dean spoke to Fred and me, as part of the incoming class of 115 students, in 1955, he said there were twenty-three applications for each admission into the first year. That was awesome! The four years of medical school, though, are largely a blur. I remember how intimidated we all were in the first year, and how inferior many of us felt to the students who came in from an honour's course in physiology or biochemistry. Somehow, I muddled through, and was ranked twelfth upon graduation. That's not a bad place to be considering that the top students, the medalists, are not always the most productive graduates in real life. In retrospect, I think that my real learning started on the day following my graduation from McGill. The patients I saw from that day onward were as much a part of my education as any text or professor I had encountered in my formal training.

Pearls

Let me now divulge "a pearl of wisdom" I wish I had known about earlier in life. The trick is about how to study, how to learn and how to remember. Here is the secret:

Learning should be viewed, not as an intellectual process; but rather, as an emotional process.

I have proven the point to my satisfaction with the following exercise, which I have used in my teaching career. I would say: "Raise your hand if you can name your favorite teacher. Keep your hand up if you can remember one fact this teacher has taught you." After a moment, the hands would come down.

"Raise your hand if you have ever been hurt by a remark made about you," I would continue. All hands would go up. "Keep your hand up if you can remember exactly what that remark was," All hands would stay up.

I remembered breaking my ankle on my driveway one winter. I remembered the loud crack, the pain, and the need to hobble back into the house. I had to go to the hospital for an x-ray and then have a below knee cast applied. I can't remember today which ankle I had broken; (I think it was the left.) but I sure remember all the hurts by different remarks made about me ever since I was a little child. And if that is so, we should take advantage of it as we try to learn or try to teach.

An event with an emotional attachment, in other words, is always remembered, and what we really learn is what we teach ourselves. That is to say, discovery or insight is always a solitary event. Learning consists of discovery, and remembering what was discovered. It might be argued that insight is an intellectual event, but if it is – that also means that insight occurs at the age of two or three, as toddlers of that age are capable of reasoning, discriminating, and abstract thinking. (When we were building a skating rink in our backyard, my two and a half year old granddaughter asked me: "Grandpa – where the tomato?" She remembered the cherry tomatoes she loved to pluck six months previously and she remembered that because the sweet taste of the tiny tomatoes made an emotional impact on her. When we associate learning with the intellect, we create problems rather than resolve them; whereas, when we associate learning with emotion, we remove barriers to learning and make the process of learning available to everyone.

Even when text-book material is taught, an emotional connection should be made. That way it will be ingrained into the mind. Mnemonic experts use hooks to facilitate memory, but if the hook is emotional, the memory will be much more lasting.

It can be argued that learning and remembering are two discrete skills; that memory is just one aspect of the learning process. I would argue that, apart from concepts in theoretical physics, ideas that appear to be difficult are just poorly conceived or poorly articulated. The average mind can grasp most concepts, but filing it into the memory bank is where the slip-up occurs.

The proposal that learning is an emotional process rather than an intellectual process was, I thought, a unique and original idea until I spoke about it to friends and colleagues. A respected scientist, Dr. Ashok Vijh, said he might have come across the idea before in the writings of Alfred N. Whitehead, and sent me a reprint of pages from his book.

While I found no reference to the topic of "emotional learning," I did discover that he had some clear views on the learning process.

Whitehead says that acquiring knowledge simply for the sake of knowledge, produces dilettantes; that the acquisition of knowledge must be purposeful or useful. I recalled that Plato had said much the same thing — that for education to be useful it must be related to the contemporary reality. Whitehead says it is unfair to test students on anything not directly taught. It struck me that I had been guilty of that. I often tested students with such exercises as: "Give me the causes of blood in the urine". I was asking for the regurgitation of text-book material. I should have asked instead:

"What illnesses have you seen during your time on our service? What did you see us do and how would you have reacted differently?"

The essence of education, according to Whitehead, must be religious. It should inculcate duty and reverence. How do you inculcate duty and reverence? You do it with repetition and more repetition, practice and more practice, again and again. Students should memorize lines from the bible, poems, sayings, lists. When Whitehead stated that learning was the inculcation of duty and reverence, the emphasis should have been be on the word "inculcation", that is, on the implantation by repetition. Every child learns the alphabet by repetition — there is no other way. The addition table and the multiplication tables are learned in much the same way. Christians memorize passages from the bible and Buddhists chant and memorize the mantras. The more knowledge is inculcated, the better the preparation for higher learning. Thus, learning multiple languages at a very young age has to be a very good thing. It is the additional alphabet or the additional multiplication table that will prepare a child for a more versatile education. The neurosurgeon, Wilder Penfield, had long championed learning multiple languages at an early age. Attempts to reduce the amount of rote learning, as is being attempted today, are wrong, dead wrong. There are no shortcuts to learning.

Professor Hebb's theory on how the mind works had a similar theme. Neural circuits that are used over and over again develop decreased resistance and become facilitated. Professor Hori, the former Zen roshi, also proposed the same thing. "Repeating the mantras over and over again is like memorizing the multiplication table," he said. The multiplication table must be memorized before more difficult concepts in mathematics can be contemplated. The basic tools must be acquired by inculcation, by repetition, by rote memorization. Inculcation of duty and reverence may be Whitehead's definition of education, but it struck me as being very close to what is taught in a Zen monastery and may be close to how psychologists perceive learning.

How does a Zen monk learn in the monastery? He learns by repetition, by rote memorization, by copying the behavior of other monks. He is not instructed on the "how" or "why" but simply on the "what." He copies what the senior monks do, feeds the many mouths, cultivates the garden, and maintains the monastery. He learns by doing, without being told what to do. He may make mistakes but he learns what is necessary.

This is what is done in surgical training as well. "See one, do one, teach one," is the way surgical techniques are learned. And when confronted with a problem, the residents are asked to solve it themselves, and not simply carry out the instructions of the senior physicians. They learn by developing their own insights!

If the teacher explains the principle and tries to force the student to remember it, the student does not develop the insight himself. Insight learning may simply not be possible if insufficient time is spent acquiring the basic tools.

Centuries ago, Aristotle said that education consists of teaching and learning, exactly in that order. That was true. Five hundred years ago Francis Bacon said "reading maketh a full man, conference a ready man, writing an exact man." He should have added *"and teaching a learned man."* In the very same essay entitled *Of Studies* which, in my estimation, is one of the best essay ever composed, Bacon goes on to say "too much time in studies is sloth; to use them too much for ornament is affectation; to make judgement wholly by their rules is the humor of a scholar... Crafty men condemn studies, simple men admire them, and wise men use them."

Today we may ask students to select the curriculum. One might fairly ask if this is wise. When we teach the details of a particular illness to a medical student, we introduce the student to a patient with the illness. The student can better remember John Smith with colon cancer than he can a patient X with the same thing. But, what I am suggesting is that we should make the process even more transparent so that students will make the emotional link more forcefully, more deliberately.

During my second year, when we were being exposed to sick patients for the first time, the professor introduced the entire class to a very attractive young woman who suffered from severe ulcerative colitis. After the details of her case were presented the professor asked the class: "Who would recommend a total removal of her large bowel with a terminal ileostomy?" We could not picture this vibrant and beautiful young woman with a permanent bag on her tummy, and none of us voted for the operation. The professor then said: "You have all condemned this young woman to a certain death!" It was a lesson we could not easily forget.

The idea that learning is an emotional process strikes me as being very Zen. The more thinking you bring into the process, the more interfering thoughts enter in as well. The more a student worries about passing a test, for example, the less he is going to know.

I have had a number of outstanding teachers in my life: in the war camps, in the public schools of Montreal, in the undergraduate program at McGill University, in medical school, and in surgical training. It is only when I am asked to specify what exactly it was I learned from whom, that I run into difficulties. What I recall instead is how a teacher performed, and how he behaved, not what he taught. For example, I remember an Endocrinologist, Dr. Martin Hoffman, who had a enviable reputation as a teacher. Nobody skipped his lectures.

At the beginning of every one of his lectures, he always had a tete-a-tete with a few students sitting up front.

"Now, were we supposed to be talking about the parathyroid today, or was it the thyroid, or the adrenal?" he would ask.

"The thyroid, sir," the students would say.

"Good," he said, and he would expound on the thyroid for the next hour.

When I think about it now, I believe it was all an act. I think he knew he was supposed to talk about the thyroid, but it was more impressive to introduce the subject that way. The sheer theatrics of his lectures made an emotional impression that was hard to forget. I have to admit, though, that what was transmitted was his eloquence, as opposed to his content.

I can't recall one scientific fact I learned from the McGill professor who encouraged me to become a urologist but I will always remember a visit we made together to see a patient in consultation. The patient was foul-mouthed, abusive, insulting, and altogether nasty to the man I admired and revered. The professor listened intently, asked his questions, examined him thoroughly, and treated the totally 'disgusting' patient, with the utmost respect. I learned something that day.

My professor at Queen's had a reputation as a skilled surgeon, but I don't remember any surgical tricks he taught me. I will, however, never forget his admonition. "In our line of work it is very easy to stretch the truth, to lie to a patient. But once you do that it will become hard to know where and when to stop, and you will not be able to remember what you said to whom. On the other hand, if you always speak the truth as you understand it you will never have to worry about what you said." It is an admonition that I carry with me to this day. I will not knowingly lie to a patient. I would prefer to support him in a bad situation, than to pretend that the situation does not exist at all.

By the time I was in my fourth and final year of medical school I was certain I would train in a surgical discipline. With my background in art and clay sculpture I thought that Plastic Surgery might be the right specialty for me. As a prelude to that, I thought of applying for an internship in Hawaii. I had never been there, but its geography and its people seemed ideal for my background. I thought that being oriental, Japanese-Canadian, in particular, I would prosper there among a clientele that was largely oriental. I was mistaken about this. My ethnicity was never an issue in medical practice. I was persuaded against going to Hawaii by family members who were appalled that I was interested in becoming a playboy and working in a field that didn't save lives. I knew better, but agreed to stay home and serve my internship at the Royal Victoria Hospital in Montreal. I then applied to the surgical training program at McGill.

Two Wistful Smiles

First though, I was entitled to a month's vacation so I chose to spend it as a camp doctor in the Laurentian mountains, not far from where I had worked as a bell-hop eight years previously. I had applied for the position towards the end of my rotating internship, never having had anything resembling a month's holiday since I had started high school. The camp had asked Dr. Phil Hill, one of the most beloved physicians of the hospital and chief of a medical service that bore his name if I had the right credentials for the job.

"I told them that of all the doctors training in our hospital the person most qualified to serve as a camp doctor would be someone who had just finished a rotating internship," Dr. Hill said to me. He then chuckled to himself as he wandered off without further explanation. I wondered why Dr. Hill would so deliberately deceive the camp officials. I knew him as a man of integrity who commanded more respect than almost any other physician at the hospital. The truth dawned on me many years later. It was true that at the end of a rotating internship I had a broader grasp of medicine than at any other time in my life.

Being a camp doctor, though, was one of the most boring undertakings a doctor could assume. I was hired in case of a catastrophe that was never meant to happen. Actually, one incident of some consequence did occur. A nine year old girl fell off a bicycle and injured her wrist. I examined her, thought she might have broken her scaphoid (a small bone in the wrist) and took her to the community hospital in town for an x-ray. The sister nurse at the hospital was very helpful. When the films had been developed, I diagnosed a hair-line fracture and told the sister that we would apply a cast. She took us to the plastering room where I completed the procedure just as I had learned it in medical school.

Later, when the parents of the young girl heard what had transpired, they rushed to the camp to fetch their daughter so that she could be examined by a prominent orthopedic surgeon in Montreal. X-rays were retaken, the old and the new films examined at length, with some debate whether or not there was a fracture. More doctors were called in before it was concluded that there was indeed a hair-line fracture. The orthopedic surgeon then said the cast had been appropriately applied and need not be touched.

The parents of the youngster were dumb-founded and wrote a letter of apology to the camp owners, confessing that they did not realize the level of medical expertise offered at the camp. The camp owners subsequently wrote a letter of appreciation to the Royal Victoria hospital, which is how I learned of the story. A small example, perhaps, but it shows the low esteem in which new physicians were held in those days.

It is too bad that the rotating internship has disappeared from the medical landscape, although it can be argued that the clinical clerkship of the fourth year amounts to the same thing. Unfortunately, this means that we have effectively reduced medical school to a three-year program. It is sad, in a way, because some of the most treasured memories I have of my years of training, occurred during my year of internship.

The ambulance duties accompanying this post, contributed more anecdotes than any other work I had during these years. At the time, only someone with a medical degree could pronounce a body dead, even if the body had been lifeless for days. I remember riding to the waterfront because a body had been found. The rotund body was sprawled on a kitchen chair, clad in knee length gumboots, jeans, and the red and black plaid shirt of a hunter. The face was white on one side, mauve on the other. The purple was due to oxygen deprived blood in his circulation, while the white was due to the maggots that covered the other half of his face. I thought I was expected to apply my stethoscope to the obviously dead body but the kind police officer said I needn't bother. This was one of the more grotesque, but easier decisions I was called upon to make, and while I was repulsed by the sight, I was, nevertheless, grateful for the easy decision-making. On another occasion, I was called upon to pronounce dead, a body found in an upper flat in the seedy section of the city.

"Two flights up!" the police officer called out.

I bounded up the creaky stairway, noticing a sign that said 'fifty cents a night', on the way. Sure enough, there lay an emaciated old man, curled up on a cot, covered only by a tattered blanket.

"I guess he's dead all right," I said to the policeman coming up behind me.

"No, doc, not him, the stiff's over there!" he said.

And, sure enough, there was a cold body on another cot, not ten feet away. These long dead bodies were not the problems however; the difficulty was with the freshly dead. We raced through the city streets to a dress factory, not unlike the shop in which my mother worked, I surmised. A middle-aged, overweight woman was slumped over, her face flat on the tabletop of a commercial sewing machine. Her body was warm. I could feel no pulse; nor could I detect any heartbeat or breath sounds when I applied the stethoscope. Could I be mistaken? Could a generous layer of fat hide a heartbeat or still the sounds? I listened again. Silence still. I looked into her eyes. The pupils were widely dilated. I pronounced her dead although I was not nearly as confident as I pretended to be. It is interesting to note that the diagnosis of death can be as confounding as the diagnosis of disease, when you are a new physician with little field experience.

The Internship

My formal internship started in surgery, on the cardiac service, with Dr. Arthur Vineberg. He was a pioneer in developing procedures to bring blood flow to heart muscles, deprived of a normal circulation because of a clot in the arterial flow. The muscles could be revitalized, he proposed, by inserting a new blood vessel, like the non-vital internal mammary artery, lying nearby. His operation would be supplanted by the by-pass procedure wherein a vein graft is stitched from the main artery of the body, the aorta, to the coronary artery beyond the site of the blockage; but the principle of heart re-vascularization started with Vineberg. He was a solitary figure, and I sometimes wonder if this trait deprived him of many awards and prizes, which he richly deserved; in fact, I wonder whether we all too often judge the book by its proverbial cover.

Am I suggesting that it is personality, and not accomplishment, which is what wins awards? Not really. What I meant to suggest was that no matter how outstanding the accomplishment, a nomination for an award would not be put forward in favor of a person who was not widely liked nor admired. When I was scrubbing to assist Dr. Vineberg's case, he smiled benignly as he stood besides me.

"What case are you scrubbing for?" he asked.

"Your case, sir," I replied.

"Have you ever scrubbed for a cardiac operation before?" he asked.

"No sir," I replied.

"That's all right," he replied. "You will do as I say."

He made me hold my two hands together, on top of the surgical drapes.

"Just stay like that and don't move!" he commanded. It wasn't long, however, before he discovered he could use me to better advantage and I was soon opening and closing the chest with his full approval. And, much later, I looked after him as my patient, for his long standing urethral stricture following prostate surgery. In fact, he would not let any other urologist touch him. Once again, the past had given me a present opportunity, and I saw visible evidence that we are all connected in some way.

Dr. Anthony Dobell was the young cardiac surgeon on the service. Once, after he had made an opening into the heart he asked me to poke my finger inside, so that I could feel the valves damaged by rheumatic fever. Allowing me to touch the damaged valves meant a significant extra blood loss, and most surgeons would not have allowed a junior resident to carry out such a move. I resolved then, that if I were ever to became a surgeon in a teaching institution, I would remember what Dr. Dobell did for me that day and that I would try to do the same for a young and enthusiastic student.

Being a junior doctor on a surgical service was very hard work, with extremely long hours, but that did not discourage me from pursuing surgery as a career. My partner on the rotation detested surgery. He was just fulfilling his commitment before he began his residency training in Internal Medicine. Once, as he poked his head into the operating room, where he was supposed to be, the attending surgeon barked at him:

"You'd better get in here. You'll never see another case like this in your lifetime."

My partner replied. "Well, sir, if I'm never going to see another case like that, need I bother?" On another occasion, we were both scrubbed on a routine gall bladder operation. Suddenly, there was a foul fecal odor, and the surgeon said:

"Oh, oh, I think we have injured the bowel somewhere." We spent the next hour searching, unsuccessfully, for a bowel perforation before we closed the incision. Later on, my partner confessed to me:

"I passed gas but I was afraid to admit it."

When I was on the Obstetrics service, my name appeared repeatedly as the person who delivered the baby on the private service. In fact, my name had appeared because a busy gynecologist had broken her wrist and could not do the deliveries with a cast on her arm. She asked me if I would do them for her, with her coaching me every step of the way. Of course, I jumped at the opportunity. I thought that perhaps she was supposed to call upon her own colleagues when she was disabled, but if she trusted me, I was not going to betray that trust. Fortunately for me, the deliveries were all uncomplicated. A junior intern was not supposed to deliver babies on the private service. His role was to notify the attending doctor on time. When I was called on the carpet by the chief of service. I apologized and said I would try harder, but I must admit, my apology was lukewarm at best!

On the medical service, I was teamed with Fred Lowy, my friend from undergraduate days. We worked hard and learned a lot, but our minds were made up as far as our careers were concerned — Fred would go medical, into Psychiatry, and I would go surgical, into Urology, as it turned out. At any rate, when I returned from my month as a camp doctor to start my surgical training, I was disappointed to learn that my first rotation was to be on the Urology service. As a medical student I had viewed the specialty as one dominated by strange instruments, long tubes, foul-smelling urine and far removed from the scalpel, scissors, forceps, and needle driver I associated with real surgery. Still, I was full of energy and was willing to put forward my best effort.

The few months I spent on the Urology service convinced me that I should consider a career in the field. The urologists appeared to enjoy their work, they were beloved by their patients, and they were kind and patient with a novice like myself. I was particularly impressed with the Roman Catholic chief of service, Dr. Kenneth MacKinnon, who exuded a quiet confidence, an imperturbability, and a genuine scholarship. When I inquired about a career in Urology he was highly supportive.

"If you like working with scopes, I think you will be happy with this discipline," he said.

And, then and there he planned my future. 'I should go to a smaller hospital to get in more "cutting" experience' he thought, so Dr. MacKinnon arranged for me to have a year of general surgical training at St. Mary's Hospital, Montreal's English-speaking Roman Catholic health care facility.

The year at St. Mary's was a pivotal one for me. At the time, residency training was hospital-based and the large university hospitals attracted the best residents. Foreign medical school graduates who wanted training in Canada ended up in university affiliated hospitals, like St. Mary's. The Catholic hospital was a haven for applicants from Mexico, South America, Haiti, Dominican Republic, Iran, Italy, India, and Korea. Often, the most formidable obstacle for the doctors-in-training was the English language. In this milieu, an English-speaking resident from McGill showed better, perhaps, than he actually was. It was a confidence-builder for me. I carried out procedures I would never have been allowed to do at the larger, university hospitals, and I recall the chief surgeon, Dr. Jack Dinan, speaking to me after my first gastrectomy. (partial stomach removal for ulcers)

"Now, Dr. Taguchi, how many of these have you done?" he asked.

My wife, Joan, in Bermuda (Oct. 1990)

"That was my first one, sir," I said and smiled inside, when I saw Dr. Dinan's mouth drop.

That was the year I came into my own as an adult male as well. I partied more often than I had ever done before in my life. I also had the good fortune to meet the lady who was to become my wife and the mother of our four children. Joan Hogan was the evening supervisor at St. Mary's, a nurse from Newfoundland who had worked in New York City before coming to Montreal. We met at the wedding party of one of the Korean residents, and became an "item" thereafter. I didn't know then that her grandfather had received a medical degree in

Baltimore, from the institution that was to become Johns Hopkins. Nor did I know that she had two brothers, both pharmacists in Newfoundland. Her mother was a war bride, having come over from London, after she had met her future husband in a London hospital when he was recuperating from injuries sustained in Gallipoli during World War I.

Joan's mother had no idea how different and difficult her life would be in Newfoundland compared to her sheltered life in London. She was not a complainer, though, and made the most of it.

My father and mother on their 50th anniversary (1979)

A more wonderful and generous person would be hard to find, and our children are better people because of her early influences. She came to help my wife with every new addition to our family.

My mother too, had no idea how her life would be in Canada. She was the only daughter of a successful businessman, and could have had a comfortable life in Japan. She had no hesitation, however, about joining the dashing young man who wanted to take her on an adventure in a foreign land.

I have enormous admiration for my mother and my mother-in-law, both comfortable at home yet willing to take on new challenges. I often wonder if I would have had the courage to pack my bags and start life in a foreign, seemingly, more backward land.

Joan's father was an advisor to Joey Smallwood, the premier of Newfoundland and a friend of Dr. James McGrath, the health minister credited for wiping out tuberculosis, in the land that was to become Canada's tenth province.

When I started my Urology training the following year, I was a confident, almost cocky upstart. Urology, which had to do with the urinary and genital diseases of men as well as the urinary disorders of women, was beginning to assert itself as an academic discipline, with exciting progress in the areas of dialysis and transplantation in the management of kidney failure. In 1958, Ken MacKinnon, the urologist, and Joe Luke, the highly regarded vascular surgeon of the hospital, had carried out the first identical twin kidney transplantation in the British Commonwealth, and with that success, the department of Urology launched an inquiry into the problems inherent in kidney failure. The Royal Victoria had already been one of the very first hospitals to try out Dr. Willem Kolff's new artificial kidney. The other institutions that were among the first four to test the Dutchman's crude contraption outside of the Netherlands, were in London, New York city, and Krakow, Poland. (The original machine sits in storage in the attic of the private pavilion of the Royal Victoria hospital.)

Ken. MacKinnon was an outstanding clinical urologist but, by his own admission, had no exposure to basic science research; therefore he invited an Oxford-trained physician to direct research in his home territory, and appointed him to a position of honour within his department. Dr. John Dossetor placed McGill Urology on the international stage as he struggled with young doctors, like Doug Ackman, Stan Lannon, and myself, among others, to carry out meaningful research. What made it all possible was a large grant from the McConnell family who owned Montreal's largest circulation English language newspaper, The Montreal Star.

In my first year of Urology training I proposed using the small intestine as a kidney substitute, when it didn't have to process food. The small intestine was interrupted at two points, at its start and at its end. Each lower cut end was brought out to the skin to form an opening or stoma, and the upper cut end was rejoined to the bowel a short distance down, in what is known as a Roux-Y anastomosis. Food would be processed by the slightly shortened bowel, and would not regurgitate out the opening to the skin, because of the normal one-way traffic in the intestines, known as peristalsis. Between meals, dialyzing fluid, or tap water containing sugar and salts to mimic the chemistry of normal serum, could be dripped into the upper opening and sucked out at the lower end. As the fluid traveled down the intestinal tract it would interact with the fluid just inside the lining of the bowel, wash out waste products that had accumulated in the blood and restore the body chemistry. A proposal to use the lining of the small intestine as a dialyzing membrane was not new; half its length as an isolated loop had been tried before with limited success. The isolated bowel normalized the blood for a short time until the blood under the lining turned into a minor lake and no longer worked as a dialyzing membrane. The proposal to use virtually the entire length of small bowel in continuity so that it processed food when it was not acting as a dialyzing membrane was new. The intestinal loop normalized the fluid volume as well as the salts and acidity, but failed to remove adequate amounts of uric acid and creatinine, two waste products that accumulate in the blood when the kidneys fail. This limited its usefulness. The procedure, christened the Taguchi loop, by Dr. David Saunders, was tried in other hospitals as well as in other cities and brought me considerable notoriety. Despite the fact that the overall result was less than optimal, my future in the field of academic medicine was assured.

I was farmed out to Queen's university, in Kingston, Ontario, for my second year of training. Dr. Andrew Bruce, a Scotsman from the Institute of Urology, London, was the chief there and the two department heads had some kind of an agreement. A third year of clinical training was deemed unnecessary, and I was sent into the laboratory instead. I should state that I was party to this agreement. I suspect I may be the only licenced urologist in North America with only two years of formal urological training.

A kidney transplantation program using fresh cadavers as organ donors, had been launched at the Royal Victoria hospital, but the rejection rate was unacceptably high. John Dossetor reasoned that the way to study the rejection process was to use a reproducible animal model involving organs, rather than a skin graft. Dr. Sun Lee, at the Scripp's Clinic in La Jolla California had devised a way of transplanting rat kidneys from one animal into another, using only optical loops, a sort of magnifying glass strapped to the head, as aids to carrying out the delicate surgery. I was sent to La Jolla, with Dr. Lee's approval, to learn the procedure. I mastered the technique, but it remains, in my mind, one of the most challenging surgical tasks I have ever encountered. Other urologists must have thought so too because

Dr. Robert Jeffs, then chief of Urology at the Hospital for Sick Children, in Toronto, offered me a staff position in Toronto simply on the strength of watching me operate on a rat. The late Dr. Willet Whitmore, then chief of Urology at Memorial Sloan Ketterling in New York city watched me do the transplant as well and said it was one of the most remarkable surgeries he had ever witnessed. Remembering these events constantly reminds me of the importance of the emotional aspect of learning.

The science of cellular immunity was in its infancy then, and even the basic terminology was confusing, as new mediators were being announced at breakneck speed. These chemicals are now called cytokines and their chemistries are more fully understood, although far from completely.

When a kidney from one inbred stain of rat (Brown Norway) is transplanted into another inbred strain (Lewis), the rejection process is complete in ten days. Experiments to modify the rejection process can then be carried out with expectations of reproducible results. (I was so preoccupied with laboratory rats that when my wife gave birth at about this time, she asked, facetiously: "Are you sure you don't want to name the baby 'Lewis'?") In my doctoral thesis I postulated a modification of the rejection process so that the recipient rat lived without immuno-suppressive drugs, and with the transplant as its only kidney for more than a year; the normal life-span of a rat, being about two years. When the modification process was tried in dogs, it failed miserably. I had discovered, it seemed, a principle that worked only in rats. It was enough to discourage me from a life in basic research.

Years later, after I was firmly established in clinical practice, I wondered about using a human fetal kidney as a donor organ. I knew that fetuses of about twenty weeks gestation were being aborted with drugs known as prostaglandins. I was also aware that the Royal Victoria was the institution which carried out these abortions, with patients coming from across the province; and, I knew these fetal kidneys were producing urine. The head nurse on the floor which cared for these women was a friend, so I asked her if she would keep some of these aborted fetuses in a bucket of ice cold saline solution. She was happy to cooperate, as these products of conception were routinely discarded in the hospital incinerator. I dissected out the kidneys from these fetuses and found them to be remarkably like the kidneys of laboratory rats in size and appearance. I transplanted a human fetal kidney into a laboratory rat just as I had done it from rat to rat and demonstrated to my satisfaction that the procedure was technically possible.

I then proposed to transplant a human fetal kidney into the wrist of a terminally ill patient, who would volunteer for the experiment to test its feasibility. The procedure proposed would involve freezing the arm, opening the skin near the wrist and forming a connection of the fetal renal artery to the radial artery in the wrist, connecting the fetal renal vein to the cephalic wrist vein, and opening the tiny ureter to the skin. After some time, a second operation might be necessary to remove the kidney. I talked to a number of terminally ill patients and they were all enthusiastic about volunteering for the experiment. Their response was heart-warming.

The project was then reviewed by the hospital ethics committee. The committee of five or six doctors listened to my proposal and unanimously declined to support the project. I said that I would respect their decision, but went on to say that if at any time or any place, someone carried out this project, I would publicly announce that I had proposed this project on this date and that I would name the doctors who stopped me from proceeding. At that point I was asked to leave the room and when I was called back the committee asked me whether permission for three would be enough. I thought three would be sufficient for a preliminary study and made plans to proceed when I was told to appear before another ethics committee meeting, now at the university level.

This panel of academics first asked me to obtain permission from the mother of the unborn child.

I found it hard to believe that they would want me to honour a woman who was ready to kill her fetus, but the committee would not budge from its stand. In addition, they wanted me to obtain permission from the father; a relative impossibility, considering the fact that in many cases, even the mother did not know his identity.

"Dr. Taguchi," another committee member said, "are you prepared to have your car bombed, your house set on fire, and your children abducted?"

I was not prepared for the reactions of outraged citizens, and dropped the project. When I submitted a report on the technical feasibility of using a human fetal kidney for transplantation, the paper was rejected by the national medical journal. The comments of the referees were sent to me, and I was floored by the anger and revulsion expressed by the adjudicators. "To what depth was the venerable old university descending when it permitted such an immoral project?" one reviewer wrote.

The use of fetal tissues to restore health in crippling illnesses is now being debated again, with the emergence of embryonic stem cells as progenitors of a repair process. I don't pretend to know what is right or wrong here but I do wonder if experts in medical ethics, no matter what their training, can render decisions that are at all meaningful. In my opinion, a universal law on ethical issues, such as the termination of a pregnancy, or the use of fetal tissue or embryonic stem cells cannot be made, because what is right for one set of circumstances is wrong for another.

Learning Revisited

I have been a student and a teacher my entire adult life. I can't recall ever getting instructions on *how* to study when I was a student. It was always *what* to study and *what* to learn, which was stressed. Actually, we do show children how to learn, when they are in kindergarten. We make the children sing a,b,c, over and over again. We follow the same process in the early years in school mathematics as well.: $2 + 2 = 4$; $4 + 4 = 8$. Repetition and rote memorization is how it is done. But, by high school, we no longer believe these core processes are that important.

Consider, as an example, the teaching of world history. How should a student tackle an assigned text of a thousand pages? Should he simply read it through twice? Should he highlight certain passages or try to form a synopsis every ten pages or so? Should he glance over the headings or look for summaries before tackling the chapter? Would reading another book on the same subject by a different author be more useful? And what should the teacher do? Read passages from the text as I recall my teacher did; prepare the summaries or assign a project based on the period? We simply do not know what works best! I contend that unless passion is brought into the process, nothing will be remembered.

Over the years, I have tried to inspire my students to work not only harder, but more effectively. This is because I believe in their inherent worth and in their ability to learn the requisite skills. It is my responsibility to tell them that they are as gifted as any author they might read and, at the same time, to guide and encourage them in their search for knowledge. I wish my teachers had done as much for me when I was younger.

"When you come across a book that does not captivate, intrigue, or inspire you, put aside that book. A textbook is supposed to arouse your curiosity, simplify, and clarify matters. If a classification does not add insight or help you to remember, it doesn't deserve your attention. Some of you are best served by the eight-hundred page textbook, which you peruse quickly to glean the salient points, while some of you are more comfortable with the two hundred page text, which you read more slowly, more deliberately." I have quoted Francis Bacon before and he says it much more eloquently: *"Some books are to be tasted, others to be swallowed, and some few to be chewed and digested — that is, some books are to be read only in parts, others to be read, but not curiously, and some few to be read wholly, and with diligence and attention."*

"Remember," I tell the students, "not one teacher in the medical faculty was appointed because of his ability to teach. We are here because we acquired expertise in a highly selected area and our example, hopefully, will bring honor to the institution. We were assigned to teach, because somebody has to do it. Your needs do not rate very high in the scheme of things." (This last remark always elicits a chuckle.)

I have also tried to improve my own teaching skills by attending seminars on how to teach. An instructor once said: "Remember, in a ten minute presentation, your audience is expected to take home three points, at most."

I raised my hand: "How did we all manage to get through medical school?" I asked.

The instructor shot back: "What makes you think you all deserved to pass!?"

Touche!

Oral examinations are notoriously subjective. The impression one creates may be more important than the knowledge one displays. When I faced the exam to defend my Ph.D thesis I was asked a question about steroid chemistry. I hadn't a clue, but I had the presence of mind to reply: "Can we talk about this after we discuss ureteral peristalsis?"

"Are you suggesting that this is an unfair question?" the examiner asked.

"You said that, sir, not me," I replied.

I recall a student who made an appointment to see me, after having performed marginally on an oral examination. Her father had suggested she do this in order to discuss it. She asked if I remembered her.

"You're the one who came into my office, slumped down on the chair, covered your temples with your two hands, and said to me: "Boy, am I nervous." I took that as a message for me not to ask you difficult questions. You immediately took yourself out of the "A" category. A superior student would never admit that he or she was nervous. If you want to be the prize-winner, you must learn to play the game."

I should state that false confidence, or cockiness, can backfire. I recall coaching one of our better residents for his specialty exam. His answers flowed well, but his attitude was cocksure to the point of condescension. I advised him that there was no sin in humility, either. Later, he confessed to me that he had entered his examination in the wrong frame of mind, but that my words had echoed in his head, and he had changed the mode of his presentation. It is at times like these that I feel most successful, because my teaching has resulted in a positive change of behaviour on the part of my student.

If learning is an emotional process, as I have suggested, we should take advantage of that fact, both as we learn and as we teach. In a recently published book entitled "Exuberance" Kay Redfield Jamison, a professor of Psychiatry and English, argues that exuberance underlies many great human achievements, and it is an emotional outburst. Furthermore, in a recent scientific report, it was shown that electrical activity in the amygdala an area of the brain associated with emotion became more active with learning, and when this activity was inhibited by beta blockers, learning was diminished. Beta blockers are medications commonly used to lower blood pressure, as well as to decrease performance-associated hand tremors, and to abort migraine attacks. In a sense, the medication attempts to counteract too much "adrenalin" in the body. A Zen devotee should be tranquil and therefore, have less "adrenalin" interference. He should have a lower blood pressure, less hand tremor, less migraine, and learn more efficiently and more effectively. This is implied in the literature, but never stated. (Has there ever been a dim-witted samurai?)

Working for Money

I was fourteen years old when I worked for a salary for the first time. I had just completed my first year of high school and I felt certain my parents could use a contribution to the family coffers. I begged my father to get me a job where he worked, at a bedroom furniture-making factory. He succeeded, I don't know how, and I was employed to stack planks and mirror frames as they emerged from a giant sanding machine. The work was not difficult, except when the pile on top of the wagon reached a point beyond my reach and I had to throw the next piece on without damaging the wood-work. The daunting task was to stay alert, waiting for the sanded product to emerge. My partner was a middle-aged man, whose work might have been more demanding, as the planks or frames undoubtedly weighed more and were more likely to cause splinters before the sanding than after; however he could control the pace of his work as he often did, by lighting up a cigarette from time to time. I don't think he was supposed to smoke, as he did it secretly and furtively. I planned to ask him if we could trade places for a change of pace and I rehearsed a few approaches, but I always backed out. He treated me well enough, and I was afraid I might upset the applecart. Thinking about it now, I should have asked. I was paid fifty cents an hour, not a bad wage for 1948 and I worked nine hours a day, five and a half days a week. I don't know if we were breaking any child labor laws but it was not as if the work had been imposed on me — I had asked for the job.

My father's task was to cut the lumber into smaller pieces, pulling the power saw towards him, as the sawdust flew all around. The pile of sawdust grew to such proportions, that the men used it as a seat when the noon whistle blew. The panorama of open lunch boxes and rumpled work clothes, coupled with the sounds of men at ease, still occupies a warm place in my memory. It also explains why my father forever smelled of sawdust, even on weekends.

I turned my pay-check over to my father, and it was received without memorable comment or fanfare. It was as though he knew it gave me pleasure to be a contributing part of the family, yet he did not wish to dignify what he saw as a reasonable expectation of his son. I worked a second summer at the same factory but graduated into finishing and packaging. I was taught how to use an electric screwdriver to attach the back panels to bedroom dressers. I was also taught how to wrap the finished products after they had been stained, varnished and dried. This was lighter work than that of the previous summer; however, the problem was that the electric drill got extremely hot. It would have helped to have worn garden gloves, but it seemed a badge of honor to do the work without them. I switched hands when the drill got too hot but my palms were red and close to blistering at the end of every day. These experiences in the furniture factory encouraged me to stay in school. The sweat shops were not where I wanted to end up.

After finishing the tenth grade I found a job as a bell-hop in Ste. Agathe, a Laurentian summer resort sixty miles from Montreal. The hotel was called "The Chalet," and it catered to Jewish couples from New York and Massachusetts, many of them on their honeymoons. I was astounded to discover that "The Chalet" was only one of a number of "Jewish" hotels, and that, within the same town, there were other hotels with large front door signs that said "Gentiles Only." We were three bell-hops, the other two a few years older. We pooled our tips and divided them equally. Although I was the youngest of the three, I was never short-changed. I did the same job a second summer, the year I finished high school, but now I was responsible for hiring two friends to make up the threesome. As bell-hops, we did not earn as much as waiters, who were with a few exceptions, university students. They were the real-life "Duddy Kravitz's" whom Mordecai Richler later popularized, hustling to extract an extra dollar from each and every guest. At weekly amateur night they would put on a skit that began with the bunch of them prancing on stage to sing their theme song:

"Tippy, tippy, ten — tippy five,
Gotta tip us five,
Gotta stay alive,
Tippy, tippy, ten — tippy five."

Many of the waiters became prominent doctors, lawyers, professors and entrepreneurs. Perhaps the most financially successful of the lot became the founder and president of a pharmaceutical firm. He has donated millions of dollars to advance Neurology and Neurosurgery at the University of Toronto. Gordon Fox became the chief of anaesthesia at my hospital, the Royal Victoria; and we often reminisced about our time together. Jack Cohen was my medical school classmate, and he became a plastic surgeon. Syd Cutler became a prominent divorce lawyer, Art Leznoff, an Immunologist, Bernie Gordon, a Psychiatrist, Skeezix Weintraub, a Gastroenterologist, Chuck Gomberg, an Internist, Jack Wolofsky, an engineer and builder, and Judah Wolofsky, a lawyer; and this list is far from complete.

Bell-hops may have earned less, but our exposure to real life drama was just as intense. The tips we received seldom reflected the size, weight, or number of bags we carried – nor did it reflect the name brand of the luggage. It was fun to play the guessing game: this guest will tip me generously, this one miserly. I was very often wrong.

One Saturday my parents visited with my young brother, arriving in one of my father's co-worker's car. I wanted to show my kid brother the rowboats, the beach, our bunkhouse, and the guest cabins, but he wandered off on his own and found a patch of poison ivy. My parents brought me a picnic package that included freshly made sushi and I offered a piece to my waiter friend.

"What am I eating?" he asked

"Raw fish and seaweed," I replied.

"Seaweed!" he cried as he spit out the bite in his mouth. Who could have guessed how popular sushi and Japanese cuisine were going to become? In 1951 it was still too exotic for the average western palate.

Decades later, I became the urologist for one of the men who owned the resort. He spoke warmly of our relationship many years earlier, and I acknowledged my gratitude in return.

After my first year at university I ran a canteen at a copper refinery plant in east end Montreal. Public transportation to the site was available but I would have spent hours on a bus every day. I persuaded my father to allow me to purchase a second hand motorcycle, and we found a BSA 125 in the "articles for sale" column of the Montreal Star. I don't recall how much we paid for the bike, but I do remember that my father handed over hard cash. The small motorcycle traveled one hundred and twenty-five miles on a gallon of gasoline which was helpful, even though a gallon of gas cost only thirty-nine cents in that era. Today, I shudder to think that I rode the motorcycle without the benefit of a helmet or any other protective gear. I did sport an old leather jacket that once belonged to my father and I fancied myself quite the modern man. I rode the motorcycle for years to get to my classes at the university as well as on excursions to the beaches or golf courses. My young brother often rode on the back but unfortunately, that place of honour was never occupied by a young lady. I think I was more concerned for the safety of young ladies than I was for the safety of my kid brother. The truth of the matter is I was afraid that if a girl rode in back, I would lose control of the bike. To add insult to fear, not one girl I knew ever asked me for a ride. Eventually I sold it to Harvey Lupu, a medical school classmate, who later became our Pediatrician. He took it to Israel after we had finished our second year, and the motorcycle died somewhere in a middle-east desert.

The canteen we ran at the copper refinery had both a stationary and a mobile component. My partner, a quiet middle aged man, never took advantage of his senior status, as we shared the work equally. The canteen was run like a Mom and Pop shop, with twice daily deliveries of soft drinks, snacks and sweets. We each loaded up a large wagon, like a shopping cart magnified many times over, and made our rounds throughout the hot refinery, rotating our routes every day so that my morning route would be taken by my partner in the afternoon. The men would come up to the mobile canteen and order drinks and snacks. Pepsi Colas and May Wests, chocolate covered vanilla flavored cakes, were the most popular. They marveled as to how I could do the arithmetic so quickly. I did not tell them I was doing the calculation as I prepared their order, not after the presentation, as my partner did. I could process the orders very quickly and the men appreciated that. Conversely, I admired these men who were able to work so hard in the stifling heat.

That summer, I saw one man lose his arm when he got it caught in a copper rolling machine, and I saw another young man fall to his death. His face was covered in soot as he lay on the floor, but the deathly pallor was plain to see. He took in a few breaths, like a fish out of water, then stopped, and never took another. "How fragile is the human body, and how stupid to lose a life so early," I thought. Would he have survived had he not fallen head-first onto a concrete floor? I wondered whether the fact that he was rushing to get to my snack cart played any role in this tragedy. In a way, I suppose, I was taking some responsibility for events which were totally beyond my control. This was merely a precursor to the lessons that medicine would later teach me in this regard.

After my second year of undergraduate studies at McGill, I found a job as an assistant to a Japanese landscaper. We hauled heavy stones to create Japanese rock gardens in different parts of the city. My boss was small in stature but possessed enormous strength and stamina. I admired his ability to examine large boulders from every angle so as to present their best faces. I do not know what qualified him to pass as a Japanese rock garden specialist, but I admired his passion for the work. Occasionally he would consult me, but I can't say he paid any attention to my input. In any case, I never disagreed with what he perceived to be the best presentation. There were quiet times during the summer and I feared for his financial stability, but he never failed to pay me.

When the contracts dried up however, I felt guilty collecting a pay check and quit.

I found employment then as an office boy. There just was not enough for me to do, and it didn't seem right to bring out a book to read, so sleep seemed the best alternative, and I was often found with my head resting comfortably on the green blotter. It became clear to me I was not going to make it as a white collar worker.

After my third year of university, I got a job helping to make slides of brain tissue at the world famous Montreal Neurological Institute. As soon as I had completed the academic year, I walked into the Institute and asked at the front desk what I might do to work there for the summer. The kind lady was so startled at my bold request, that she sent me to speak to various people in the building instead of rejecting me outright. Before the day was over, I was hired to assist Mr. Gilbert, the lab technician, who made all the microscopic slides of brain tissue removed by the neurosurgeons. I quickly learned the trade, even the intricate silver and gold impregnation techniques, but Mr. Gilbert failed to tell me or if he did it did not register that the slides had to be prepared from the surface of the specimen identified by a little nick. For days and weeks, I made beautiful slides from the surface of the brain with no disease, on the opposite side. The error was pointed out to me by Dr. Gilles Bertrand who was a fellow then, but who has since had a distinguished career at the Institute.

I did get to meet the famous surgeons, Dr. Wilder Penfield and his associate, Dr. William Cone, both men obviously dedicated to their work. Dr. Cone would take trays of slides on his vacation and dream up different ways of staining the specimens. I don't know if it is true or not but I heard it said that he almost drowned once when he tried to rescue slides that had tumbled out of his boat. Dr. Penfield was world famous for his pioneering surgery to treat epilepsy and for mapping the functions of the cerebral cortex. He also, I believe, enjoyed his notoriety. I watched him operate because the main operating room in the institute was fitted with an observation deck. He must have mistaken me for a visiting dignitary because he went out of his way to describe what he was doing. I kept nodding as if I understood what he was saying and hoped he wouldn't recognize me later as his summer lab technician. When I read his autobiography, years later, I was pleased to learn that had he not become a neurosurgeon he would have chosen Urology as his specialty.

During my final year in undergraduate studies, I was employed by the department of Psychology, where I was completing studies for an honor's degree. Exciting research projects were underway in the department with Jim Olds and Peter Milner discovering the "pleasure center" in the rat brain and Woody Heron, working on "sensory deprivation." Both projects arose from professor Hebb's theory about how the brain worked, and ante-dated Ron Melzack's seminal publication, called "The Puzzle of Pain." I was employed to run the sensory deprivation experiments. Volunteer subjects were confined to a tiny chamber the length and width of which were the size of single bed mattress, with a height that did not allow any subject to stand. The volunteer wore cuffs that extended beyond the finger tips, on his arms, in order to deprive him of his sense of touch. Foggy goggles to deprive him of normal sight, and plugs in his ears to eliminate hearing completed the deprivation package. Electrodes were then placed on his scalp to record the brain waves. Periodically, measurements were made of his basal metabolic rate. My role was to observe the subject from outside the chamber, feed him, take him to the bathroom, and carry out elementary tests; taking the pulse and measuring the blood pressure. I remember one football player who thought it was meal time every two hours, and he asked for a half a dozen eggs with toast at regular intervals. A medical student who later became a professor of surgery lasted the longest — five full days! Another student volunteer became deranged and had to withdraw from medical school. It was not clear if his confinement in the experiment had contributed to his health problem. At first the investigators did not believe that all the subjects were hallucinating. They thought the volunteers were simply contriving to maintain contact with the outside world. I remember one subject who saw rabbits jumping out of a golf bag, which suddenly turned into a shotgun. One of the investigators became a volunteer subject himself, hallucinated, and from that point onward, this manifestation became part of the formal test results. I did not attend any lectures during the time I worked on the project, but I had access to the professors' notes. I don't think the job interfered with my academic performance but I do believe it is responsible for one recurring nightmare that haunted me for years. In the dream, I must sit a university course examination and I realize I have not attended a single lecture nor read one page of the text. I am sweating profusely, debating to myself whether I should attempt the exam, an advanced chemistry course, or skip it and face the consequences. At that point, I awaken with a start. I wonder why this nightmare became a part of my life. Perhaps it hearkened back to my disastrous first year in the war camp, but in retrospect, it might be better to simply attribute it to stress, the accepted villain for all of today's ills.

The summer I graduated with a Science degree, I was employed by the department of Psychology. I don't know if my professors in Psychology were aware that I had applied to medical school. They tried to interest me in a graduate program in Psychology, and I feigned some interest because I didn't know if I would be accepted into Medicine. I must admit that once I had received my acceptance, my work output dropped sharply, despite the fact that my time sheet remained the same. I carried out different projects, some involving Scottish terriers. Earlier experiments had shown that dogs kept in isolation for a protracted period lost their ability to solve simple problems, like running around barriers to find food. The dogs had long passed their period of isolation and no longer had a problem with the maze, but we had fun trying to get the dogs to behave stupidly for a documentary film.

Today, medical students get little time off during the summer and spend more time in "electives" at different institutions around the world. They pay the expenses. In my time (1955-1959), we got two months off during the summer. I figured two months was insufficient time for any income generating activity, let alone to secure any job. This may have been a miscalculation because professor Clermont, who taught the Histology course offered me a Summer job, which I had to decline, when I was a first year student. I often wonder how different my life might have been had I been in a position to accept that offer. Might I have become an anatomist, or a pathologist? I had joined the reserve force of the Canadian Air Force at the beginning of my medical studies and, as a cadet, I was assured a summer job. I spent one summer in Ottawa, the second in Edmonton, and got the prized overseas posting the third summer.

I always had trouble distinguishing right from left as, I suspect, left handed people are more apt to do. "Right turn!" the drill sergeant would bellow out, and I would turn left, thus causing not only a break in the flow, but a 'ten-pin' fall in the ranks. One day, I ran across the drill-master on the camp grounds. I stopped and gave him a sharp salute. He took me aside, put his big arm around my shoulder and told me he was a non-commissioned officer. An officer-in-training, he explained, does not salute a sergeant. I replied that as long as I marched the way I did and as long as he was my drill master I would continue to salute him whenever our paths crossed. He smiled and gave me an undeserved mark in "drill." In short, I had been rewarded for saluting a non-commissioned officer. Not too bad for a directionally-challenged summer recruit!

The summer posting was to One Fighter Wing, in Marville, France. The base was near the Belgian border and this was 1958, the year of the International World Fair in Brussels, so I got to see the World Fair; the modest Canadian contribution, and the colossal US and Russian pavilions. The most exciting experience for me that summer, however occurred on a trip to Amsterdam.

We were five cadets, four guys and a gal. The lady was a student in Sociology, engaged to be married soon to a protestant minister. When we reached Amsterdam in our rented car, it was our lady companion who shouted out:

"Hey, that looks about our speed!" referring to a nearby hotel. We did not know that we were in the middle of the red light district. Our lady student retired for the night and the four of us broke up into pairs for a walk around the block. My companion was an engineering student from Manitoba and when we returned from our walk we settled for a beer at the bar, where we watched in fascination as the ladies of the establishment draped themselves all over their male companions. We ordered more beer.

Suddenly, through the front door of the establishment, in marched an officer of the US military, in full regalia.

"I must speak to the proprietor of this establishment," he demanded.

Eventually, the proprietor materialized.

"I have reasons to suspect the girls of this hotel are diseased, and if they are, I must know because my men have been exposed," he said.

The proprietor protested.

"My girls are all clean," he claimed.

"They must agree to be examined'" the officer said.

"No way!" the girls of the establishment replied in unison.

"If you wish, I can have the medical officer come here," the officer said.

It was at this point my companion from Manitoba spoke up.

"Hey, no problem, we have a doctor in the house!"

"Are you a doctor?" the officer asked as he approached me.

"No," I replied, "I'm just a medical student."

"Can you tell if a girl is diseased?" the officer demanded.

"Not always, unless it's very obvious," I said, hesitantly. (I wonder why I didn't say I had no skill whatsoever to make such a diagnosis. I would say so today but when you are young you are less willing to confess your inadequacies.)

"No way I am going to permit any half baked doctor carry out examinations," the proprietor said.

The American officer stormed out in a huff.

Somehow, the girls of the establishment surmised that the young Canadians had bailed them out of a difficult situation. They wanted to reward us by 'entertaining' us without charge, in our room. We were afraid of disease, as well as the reaction of our soon-to-be-married lady companion and declined their offer. The girls viewed this as further evidence of our angelic nature and invited us to see the city with them in the morning.

Sure enough, the following morning the ladies, now properly attired, accompanied us on a city tour. Our Sociology student picked out her trousseau with the help of the women and, to this day, I am certain she does not know her wedding dress was purchased with the help of the prostitutes of Amsterdam.

Research

I have had just one professional job in my entire career — that of urologist at a large university hospital in Montreal. It is, I think, a prestigious job, but it was not a position I particularly coveted. It was just handed to me when I was ready to start working, and I accepted it without much deliberation. In fact, a friend gave the matter more thought than I ever did. He was an American, just a year ahead of me in training, but a few years older because he had served in Korea. He called me from Seattle when he heard that I was accepting a position at McGill and its teaching hospital, the Royal Victoria.

"Yosh," he said, "you must reject the offer from McGill. You don't belong in that Anglophile institution. You're not a Mic or a Mac, there's no future for you there. Turn down the offer and come and work with me."

I knew my friend meant well but I was a little suspicious. Maybe he coveted the offer that was never made to him. I tried to be polite and told him I was going to try it out and see how it went. Over the years I have come to appreciate just how political medical jobs are and how genuinely kind my friend was, in inviting me to come down and to work with him.

Some of this reality hit home when I applied for a staff position at a university-affiliated hospital, St. Mary's, where I had done a year of surgical training before I started my formal work in Urology. I thought I had been a noteworthy resident at that hospital, more scholarly and certainly more articulate than many of my fellow residents from non-English speaking parts of the world. Furthermore, I had married the nurse who was the hospital's evening supervisor and that, I thought, should figure into the equation. I have come to realize that institutions pay little attention to personal details when a new appointment is made. Curriculum vitae may be examined, endorsements checked, but the bottom line is: "Will this candidate fill our needs?"

My appointment to the Royal Victoria carried admitting privileges, but I was expected to devote substantial time and effort to basic medical research. I couldn't imagine clinicians sending me patients when I was so intimately identified with non-clinical activities and I figured a simultaneous appointment to a smaller hospital, was the way to get my clinical career launched. I was surprised, shocked may be closer to the truth, to get a blunt rejection. To this day, I am not certain why. Did the urologists on staff at the smaller hospital feel threatened, that I may take away cases that would normally have gone to them, that the operating room and hospital beds could not accommodate the practice of another urologist? Or, did my chief feel that such an appointment would detract from the lab work he expected me to carry out, and masterminded the rejection? Competence, I felt, was not the issue.

I was the very first full-time appointment in Urology at McGill although at the time I did not appreciate the significance of the honor. I thought it was a way to keep me in the lab and away from potential patients all doctors coveted. A full-time university appointment meant that in addition to looking after whatever patients he or she might have, the appointee was required to allot substantial time, effort, and energy to research activities, to the teaching of medical students and residents, and to administrative duties. I don't know where this scheme originated but it is pervasive across academic centers in Canada and the USA including reputable institutions like Harvard, Johns Hopkins, and Stanford. And it doesn't work. A full-time staff member is provided with a salary, secretarial help, and a rent-free office in the hospital but, there is a ceiling set on his clinical earnings. The truth is that young doctors at academic institutions moonlight because they cannot make ends meet. A prestigious appointment alone does not pay the bills.

Our society pays a doctor who treats a wealthy man much more than it rewards a scientist whose work may benefit all of mankind. I did not at the time fully appreciate the positive aspects of my full-time contract. I didn't have to worry about office rent, the hiring or firing of secretaries or office managers, nor even attracting a patient load to assure an income to meet the monthly expenses. Like other novice appointees, I complained about the negatives. The contract implied that, left to police myself, I would cheat and spend a disproportionate amount of time and energy in clinical practice. The contract was an insult to my academic integrity. If I had been interested primarily in dollars, I would have opted for private practice. The university offers a full-time contract to encourage productivity from its new recruits, but it should not rely on penalties in order to fulfill its mission. Instead, it should terminate a contract if the appointee is not productive. At least that is how I see it.

At the end of my specialty training period, I earned a Ph.D. by discovering a way for a kidney transplant to avoid rejection in a laboratory rat model, and I published a series of papers in reputable scientific journals. An early paper in which I described a way to attach a donor ureter to a recipient bladder in man, a technique I had adapted from doing the surgery repeatedly in the rat, was tested and determined by urologists in Spain, McGill, and elsewhere to be a simpler and better method than other techniques described. I thought this was a minor contribution to the urological literature and not as noteworthy as some of my other publications. I was far more proud of the proposal that the upper and lower ureter could be operated upon during the same operation without losing blood supply to the structure, or that a second blow-out (diverticulum) could be left alone when the first one was excised because it harbored a tumor. In medical science, it appears there is often no direct correlation between work and reward.

I no longer do basic science research with grants sought from the federal government, but I am often involved in pilot projects — studying an old drug for a different use, or investigating an established energy, like electricity, for a new and novel use. Let me explain.

I was intrigued by the observation that when a foreign object, like a wood splinter penetrates the skin, the body reacts to the insult with an "angry", violent response. The site of penetration swells with the accumulation of fluid and white blood cells, and the area turns red and hot. If the insult is severe enough, the lymph nodes nearby enlarge and manufacture chemicals to help fight and contain the "poison" that has invaded the body. But, when the foreign invaders are cancer cells, there is no inflammatory reaction at the site of origin, and the lymph nodes not only fail to contain the insult but rather, become fertile soil for further spread of disease. Why do the defense mechanisms fail? Are the cancer cells not "foreign" enough to encourage a foreign body reaction? Can we deliberately make the defense mechanisms of the body more active against the cancer cells, or make the cancer cells more foreign (immunogenic)? Can we assist the natural processes as they were meant to occur?

What if we were to introduce "adjuvant" to the reaction? Adjuvant is a non-specific immune enhancer. Freund's adjuvant is one example. It is composed of particulate-containing oily substances that promote protein aggregation, which when mixed with a protein that can cause an immune response, act as a tissue depot, slowly releasing the protein (antigen) that activates the immune reaction. Another established adjuvant is BCG, or Bacille Calmette-Guerin, a strain of bovine tuberculosis, that is used to vaccinate against tuberculosis as well as against certain neoplasms like bladder cancers and malignant melanomas.

Might I be able to help my patients afflicted with prostate cancer by enhancing their immune response with BCG? If the prostate cancer cells themselves do not mount a sufficient immune response, might it occur if I were to add BCG to the equation? I had just the right candidate for the experiment. My patient was failing the traditional treatments, including hormones. He was intelligent, and he was opposed to trying chemotherapy, having researched the literature. I proposed injecting BCG directly into his cancerous prostate. Attempts to treat solid tumors with BCG were not entirely new and my patient became familiar with the limited medical literature on the subject. I encouraged him to sign an elaborate consent form I had devised. Then I injected BCG directly into his prostate under ultrasound guidance. This was easy to do. I simply substituted a long hollow needle for the biopsy needle used for the ultra-sound guided biopsies, and instilled the BCG, in a regular salt solution.

My patient almost died of disseminated tuberculosis, and required intensive anti-tuberculous medications, but his cancer was contained for well over six months. I am certain the hospital ethics committee would never have approved the project, had I passed it through them; nor would they have approved the experimental surgery to use the bowel as a dialyzing membrane, I had carried out earlier in my career. Individual members on ethics committees mean well, but the authority entrusted to them sometimes distorts their sense of value, and safety concerns overtake their appreciation of science, which always involves some risk-taking. I can imagine a medical ethicists decrying this last remark but, if they are entrusted with limiting science, they must become more aware of medical facts. For example, if they were to take a stance against circumcision, it must not be because they equate it to female genital mutilation, or to Zionism as some people have done.

I am certain a way will be found to enhance the immune system of cancer victims or to make the native cancers cells more immunogenic. We already know, for example, that irradiated cancer cells processed by dendritic cells, harvested from the inner skin and cultivated in vats outside the body, produce immune responses that cancer cells alone do not. The problem with this kind of immunotherapy is that a product manufactured for one patient may not help others.

What about electricity as a cancer killing agent? I don't mean killing cancer cells with the heat generated by electricity, but rather using an electrical current to kill cancer cells selectively. Scientists have demonstrated that certain solid tumors can be killed by an electric current, so why not try the idea on prostate cancer cells grown under the skin of laboratory animals? These models already exist. All that needed to be done was to bring together the basic scientists working with the animal model and the lab people with the proper current- producing apparatus. This project has been launched in our animal research laboratory under the supervision of Dr. Simone Chevalier with the help of Dr.Ashok Vijh, the research director of Hydro-Quebec, who first proposed the idea. These pilot projects are exciting and, perhaps, one of them will produce results which will encourage more studies. Time will tell.

I am involved as well, with more mundane research, like phase-three drug trials. If a new chemical formulation shows promising results in animal studies, it enters what is called "phase one human trials." Human volunteers are paid for testing the new drug for dangerous side effects. Then, in "phase two studies" different dosages are tested. A significant number of people in several countries are then recruited for the "phase three" studies which determine whether the product can be brought to market. Despite these stringent controls, some drugs are released to market too soon, as Bayer found out with their cholesterol-lowering drug, Baycol, and Merck, with their anti-inflammatory Cox-2 inhibitor, Vioxx. It is not that the pharmaceutical firms are unaware of these risks – they remember the thalidomide disaster – but they cannot know how many volunteers need to be tested for how long before any drug can be called totally safe.

Science must always be cognizant of the wishful-thinking of its scientists. It is human nature to see a cause-and-effect relationship that is expected. Science must also account for the placebo effect of a drug. A new drug may help two out of three patients affected with a particular malady. An identical pill without the active chemical, the placebo, may improve the results in a third of patients. Unless both the doctors and the patients are blinded as to who is getting what, a scientific conclusion cannot be drawn. This is the rationale for the double-blind, placebo-controlled study, the basis for every new drug released to the public. There is no innovative input from doctors for these studies, but the pharmaceutical industry rewards the university and our specialty handsomely for recruiting candidates for them.

Medical research, in fact, takes many forms. In the classic model it follows the scientific method: propose a hypothesis, design an experiment to prove it right or wrong, and accept the conclusion.

Medical breakthroughs, however, do not occur that way most of the time. Instead, there is an accident, a serendipitous cause-and-effect observation, discerned by a trained mind. Examples of this abound. Mold contaminating a bacterial culture plate appeared to be inhibiting bacterial growth at the point of contamination, and this observation led to the development of penicillin. Cultivated tumor cells died near a platinum electrode, an observation that led to the development of platinum-based chemotherapy. A human spermatozoa deliberately placed adjacent to a woman's egg cell accidentally punctured the outer wall of the cell and resulted in a fertilization, and the launch of the *in-vitro* fertilization industry. An automobile accident causing a windshield injury to an eye corrected short-sightedness, and launched laser surgery for myopia. A drug being tested for the treatment of hypertension stimulated erections, and this was how Viagra came into being. These breakthroughs occur because people were receptive to results "outside-the-box."

It can be argued that these advances are counter-Zen; that a mind fixated on a problem is incapable of thinking outside the box; that an unexpected result might be dismissed or overlooked. On the other hand, it can be argued that the Zen mind would more likely make an observation that might have eluded a less focused mind. I believe this is the stronger argument. In the Zen world the results would speak for themselves, unclouded by wishful thinking, or distracting emotions.

Science requires statistical proof, but statistics and science are not synonymous. Too often there are reports of a scientific study "proving," for example, that operations done on Tuesday have a complication rate higher than those done on Wednesday. There may have been ten complications per thousand cases on Tuesday and five per thousand on Wednesday. This may then be reported as twice as many complications on Tuesday as compared to Wednesday. "Garbage in and garbage out" as someone has said. Science is as good as the question it is asked. Medicine is advanced by people who master what is known and unsatisfied, ask: "How can it be made better?"

Memories

Throughout my career, I have met and treated thousands of patients. While each one of them was important, some stand out in my memory as noteworthy. (Their names have been altered.)

Let me start with the story of Mr. Ben Kurtz. He was a sixty three year old man when he was first sent to me for treatment of a huge cancerous growth in his right kidney. The likelihood that the disease had already spread beyond the organ was quite high, although the chest x-ray, bone scan and brain scan all indicated no disease in these distant locations. These are the sites long recognized as areas for metastatic (spread) disease when the primary cancer is in the kidney. Surgery was the only hope.

When the kidney was exposed it became abundantly clear that tumor tissue was in the main blood flow out of the kidney renal vein as was indicated by the ultrasound examination, and that the tumor tissue extended to where this large vessel emptied into the main venous trunk called the vena cava. I clamped the vena cava, narrowing the caliber from that of a large carrot, to that of a pencil. In this way, I was able to remove the football- sized mass that had replaced the kidney. Unfortunately, all the little veins behind the kidney known as the lumbar vessels were plugged with visible grey material — cancerous tissue! There was no way I could remove all the cancer. I tidied up and closed the incision.

Ben survived the operation and defied all the odds. Now, seven years later, there is no evidence of cancer in his body. What happened to the cancer I had left behind? They were not microscopic deposits. The cancer was visible to the naked eye. Somehow, Ben's defense mechanism had killed off the cancerous cells. I wanted to test his blood to see if I could extract the protective material his body generated but, although I had Ben's cooperation I have not been able to entice a "lab" man to design the appropriate experiment.

Kidney cancers are unique. They are the only neoplasms I deal with that can run unpredictable courses. A patient can have advanced disease, like Ben, and survive. Another patient with seemingly early cancer can progress and die despite the fact that there was no sign of disease at the edges of the specimen which was removed.

Mrs. Jane Pilotte was another memorable patient whose kidney cancer had spread not only into her renal vein but into the vena cava, with tentacles extending into her heart. With the help of cardiac surgeons, and with her heart stopped, we removed all the obvious tumor and she is still alive and well, fifteen years after her surgery.

Louise McTaggart had a kidney cancer incompletely removed, I was certain of that, yet she showed no further signs of the cancer for the rest of her life; at least not in the following twenty-two years.

I removed one kidney from David Shalinsky because it harbored a cancer, and removed a small growth from the remaining kidney at the same time. I am not certain if the small growth was a spread lesion or a second primary, but he has been cancer- free since, now for over six years.

Pierre Gallagher had a gunshot injury, and the bullet went right through the renal vein, shattering both the front and back wall of the vessel. As over ten percent of all the blood pumped out of the heart goes directly to each kidney, a patient with such an injury should bleed to death within minutes if not seconds. That normally does not happen because the blood that spills into the tissue raises the resistance to further spillage, and a spasm of the artery to the kidney reduces the normal blood flow. He was in the operating room within an hour of the injury, but he had no detectable blood pressure when the operation began. I removed the kidney as quickly as I could, while the anaesthesiologist pumped in the replacement blood as fast as he was able. Mr. Gallagher survived and looked so well I could not recognize him when he made his post-op visit.

Once, I injured a pelvic vein during an operation to remove a cancerous bladder. When this happens, blood wells up in the wound like a stoppered sink filling with water when the tap is turned on full blast. Death on the operating table is a real possibility. I held my fist over the bleeding site while the anaesthesiologist pumped in all the blood he had on hand, and cross-matched him for more. After losing more blood than his entire blood volume I was able to sew up the tear and stop the deluge. Charlie Crone's recovery from surgery was uneventful despite this massive blood loss, but he never regained his energy. I searched for cancer left behind or arising anew, but all the tests were negative. Mr. Crone slowly wasted away and died three years later with terminal diarrhea. Eight years after his death I was notified that he had received HIV-positive blood. He had died of AIDS that was never suspected nor diagnosed. I had to reveal this fact to his widow who, fortunately, tested HIV-negative.

One morning, as I was beginning my scrub for a total prostate removal my resident asked if I was aware that our patient, a school teacher, was gay. I confessed that I didn't know.

"I asked if I could run an HIV test but he declined," my resident said, "do you still plan to go ahead with the operation?"

"Why not?" I said.

But, despite our extra precaution, this was the case in which my finger was pricked with a needle, and my resident was splashed in the eyes during the procedure. I turned to the anaesthesiologist:

"Please take his blood for HIV testing. I don't care what laws I may be breaking. I will assume all responsibility," I said.

After the operation I sent a letter to the hospital administration. I said I was going to hold the hospital liable if I or any member of my surgical team were HIV converted because of the hospital policy. "Allowing the patient to decline HIV testing might have made sense when there was no drug regime to delay or abort a trans-mission after exposure, but didn't make sense now," I wrote. I had a visit from the hospital lawyer who asked if I meant what I said in the note.

"If I didn't mean it, I wouldn't have written it," I said.

Fortunately for us, the test on the patient came back negative and the hospital policy has since changed. I believe we can ask for the test without permission, but the patient can decline to be made aware of the result.

I encountered one of my favorite patients in my first year in practice. Mrs. Elena Halas was pregnant for the fourth time and, at about the same time, her husband was diagnosed with schizo-phrenia. In a panic Mrs. Halas tried to abort herself with lye and vinegar as instructed by a friend. She missed the cervix, placed the strong chemicals into her bladder, and came to the hospital emergency room in agony. When the emergency doctor examined her he found a grey material extruding from her urinary opening. He clamped it in a forceps and pulled. What came out was the entire cast of the bladder lining. At that point she came under my care.

Her urethra was healthy but her bladder had shrunk down to a size of a golf ball, actually the size of the balloon of the Foley catheter which had been placed after the "cast" had been extracted. I proposed to build her a new bladder using a segment of her intestines. I have been her doctor for over thirty-five years and, although she has had periodic urinary infections she has done well. She is proud to have raised three children and leads a normal life.

I have had to perform the very same operation, this time on a gentleman, because he had a bizarre bladder disease, called eosinophilic cystitis, which makes the bladder behave as if it has been attacked by powerful chemicals. The urologist treating the patient was my former student and I felt comfortable advising him to proceed as I had done with my lady patient many years previously. He was reluctant to carry out such an uncommonly performed procedure in a community hospital and transferred the patient to my care. The patient was on heavy doses of cortisone, which delayed his recovery but he was absolutely delighted with the outcome of the operation. He told me that he had been suicidal before his transfer.

Another grateful patient had his bladder removed when he was only forty-two years old because of cancer. I deliberately left untouched a small segment of his prostate so that he might retain his potency. Now, thirty years later, he is a happy man, but his wife complains to me that I should have rendered him impotent because he will not leave her alone.

Many patients have showered me with gifts over the years. I do not have enough shelf space for all the alcoholic beverages I have received. Some however, occupy a special place in my mind.

Once, after a successful correction of Peyronie's disease, a condition in which the penis might curve as much as ninety degrees upon erection, the patient handed me a piece of paper with two words written on it.

"Put a thousand dollars on this and have a holiday on me," my patient said. "Now, don't get greedy. When it doubles, sell."

I consulted my older colleagues who seemed unconcerned about the prospect of losing a thousand dollars, but it was a significant sum for me at that point in my career. I did double my investment on my first foray into the penny stocks.

Another patient offered to build me a hospital.

"But a hospital is not like a condominium. There are municipal regulations, provincial regulations, federal laws..."

"You don't think I know all that?" he replied. "Besides, I wasn't thinking of building a hospital in Montreal. I want to build it somewhere down south where it is warm, in the Caribbean islands, perhaps..."

I thanked him but told him I had no desire to leave Montreal.

Other patients have donated money to the hospital foundation. When patients discuss a potential donation with me I ask them to contribute to my own fund, which has been used to support research activities not funded by granting boards. One patient (Avi Morrow) organized a collection from a group of friends, including himself, to provide funds to purchase a new ultrasound machine, an eighty thousand dollar item. It has a split screen so that the prostate gland can be viewed from the front and from the side at the same time, thus permitting far more accurate biopsies.

In recent years, I have been accumulating capital which I hope will become sufficient to support an academic activity, like a scholarship or a research prize. It will probably not be enough to endow a chair, as a few of my friends in business have done. Should I ever be in a position to do that, though, I don't know if I can be as modest as one of my friends was, when he described his philanthropic plans to me. He told me he was on the way to Edmonton, where he had studied earlier in his life. The purpose of his trip was to endow a chair at the local university. I registered my admiration at his ability to spend a million dollars on an educational odyssey, and he simply smiled and allowed that it was only half that amount. I suppose it was merely the proof of the old adage "Where you stand depends upon where you sit."

Rules for Life

I have described, in some detail, the various jobs I have had, and the work I do in my professional career. I believe Confucius had it almost right when he said: *Find work that is not work and you will never work another day in your life*. I say he had it almost right because it should not be "find work" but it should be "make work." <u>Make</u> *work not work and you will never work another day in your life.*

Health

A medical doctor gets no special training on how to assure a healthy life for himself. Like the proverbial cobbler whose own shoes needs repair, a doctor is better at giving advice than he is at taking it. In medical school he will learn that a gram of fat will produce nine calories while a gram of carbohydrate or protein will generate four. He will be taught that the ingestion of vitamins and trace metals are essential for life, but he will have received confusing or no instructions at all on the value of small, medium, or massive intakes of nutritional supplements. If he is a fan of organic foods and opposed to genetically modified produce, he will have developed that stance outside his formal training in school. Common sense should indicate to him that smoking is bad, and that an excess of anything is more likely to be harmful than helpful. Smoking, by the way, does not only increase the risk of lung cancer, it also promotes bladder cancer, and by constricting small blood vessels, increases the chances of heart attacks, strokes, and impotence, or ED (erectile dysfunction) as it is now called.

Not surprisingly, there are doctors who smoke, eat excessively, live a sedentary life, and die prematurely of lung cancer, diabetes, hypertension and heart attacks. Many doctors will argue that it's mostly in the genes, and that diet or lifestyle changes won't amount to much. "Remember Churchill," they'll argue. "Didn't he smoke like a chimney and drink like a fish, and didn't he live to a ripe old age?" A jogging guru actually died while running, and how many others have followed in his wake? Where is the evidence that shows an increased life span with anti-oxidants, or with any other nutritional supplement, for that matter?

The data may be scant indeed, but I am convinced anti-oxidants and exercise make a difference. If I take the trouble to rust-proof my car, why shouldn't I be as kind to my body? The process is comparable. Oxidation promotes rust on the car body, and the presence of the unnecessary oxygen (free radicals) in the body tissue promotes degenerative diseases, cholesterol deposits on arterial linings, and cancer. If these toxic molecules are absorbed by anti-oxidants, available as vitamins, why not supplement the daily diet?

Shouldn't a good nutritional diet be sufficient? Perhaps, but who actually follows the national guidelines? We live a fast- paced life and rush our meals, and we undoubtedly don't chew our food properly, as our parents constantly reminded us to do. If there are people who make certain their meals include items from the four major food categories, I don't know who they are. Furthermore, twenty oranges will be required as a substitute for one tablet containing one gram of vitamin C. It is this statement that starts many of my patients on vitamins. No matter how good their eating habits, nobody juices twenty oranges every morning.

I take one gram of vitamin C every day (Linus Pauling used to take twenty grams, remember?) along with 400 international units of vitamin E containing 50 micrograms of Selenium, and I readily admit it is not based on anything I learned in medical school. A study has just been launched in the USA and Canada to determine if the combination of Vitamin E and Selenium can reduce the risk of developing prostate cancer, but we won't know the results of that study until a decade from now. In the meantime, the study pitch argues, "don't start the supplements until you consult your doctor." Does that make any sense? Science doesn't know, so how can the doctors possibly advise?

I encourage exercises for my patients but I did not do them regularly myself. I thought that running up and down the hospital stairs, as I do, mowing my lawn, and tending my garden were exercise enough. It came as a shock for me to discover that my health, stamina, and sense of well being could be altered dramatically by vigorous exercise. I don't think it matters what activity is pursued: running, jogging, swimming, cycling, or any other active sport, as long as the heart rate speeds up to a count approaching two hundred beats per minute. In my case, it was tennis.

Marcel Einhorn, a patient first and, sub-sequently, a good friend, was convinced I would enjoy the sport. Tennis was his passion. At his regular annual visit, he would ask me when I was going to take him up on his offer for some free coaching. "Yes, one day I will do it", I kept saying, but I never did.

One day, Marcel arrived at my office with three pairs of tennis shoes.

"Try them on," he said, "One's gotta fit."

Of course one did, and I have been playing ever since; now for over fifteen years.

Marcel was not the only one who was so helpful to me. Martin Lande insisted that I play with him twice a week even though I was a beginner and totally erratic. To make me feel good he would often miss-hit the ball deliberately. I improved slowly, but then Martin developed Lou Gehrig's disease and could no longer play. He arranged for me to play with Peter Shiftel, his associate at work. Peter and I played for a number of years until Peter had to stop because of a heart irregularity. I then joined Marcel and his partner, Morel Bachynski, until leukemia suddenly claimed Marcel's life. Now I play regularly with Morel. We play six serves each, and I am pleased when I take one or, at best, two points out of the six. Winning is not the issue. Health is.

The improvement in my health from playing tennis regularly was dramatic. I used to tire after a long day in the operating room. The muscles in my legs would ache, and even if I went to bed earlier that night, I was still tired and my muscles would still be aching the next day. Now, although I am older, I am more energetic and I no longer experience these symptoms. If I had not observed these changes in myself, I could not have been convinced that exercise made such a difference.

Good health is not strictly due to a lucky genetic endowment. It is a matter of attitude, nutrition, and heart racing exercise. Attitude is important because emotions affect the functioning of the immune system. You turn it on with laughter, you turn it off with sorrow. Norman Cousins may have popularized the concept initially, but Esther Sternberg expanded the claim. She has done it with elegance in her book "The Balance Within." Esther is a native of Montreal with a medical degree from McGill. Fully trained as a Rheumatologist, I don't know where this established scientist learned to write so well, but her book was a delight to read. It cogently explored the connection that must exist between health, mind, and the emotions.

There is a plethora of products promoted to enhance the immune system. Certainly they are not harmful but it is debatable how effective they may be. After all, the immune response is likely to be enhanced if the consumer feels the product is going to help.

Obesity is due, in large measure, to an intake of more calories than the body requires and more than the body can burn off. There are some elementary facts many overweight people refuse to acknowledge. They often have an enormous intake of calories while they claim they eat next to nothing; they think excess calories can be readily burned off, and they think diets make very little sense. Actually, it is indeed very difficult to lose weight by burning off the fat. It is much easier to do so by cutting the intake. One simple formula equates 3500 calories to one pound. In other words, an intake of 500 calories less each day, should translate into a one pound weight loss at the end of one week. A booklet that tabulates the amount of calories in servings of different food-stuffs, a calorie counter, in other words, could indicate how easy it is to eliminate this 500 calories a day. Lowering the caloric intake by cutting down the carbohydrate, rather than the fat or the protein constitutes the basis of the Atkins diet. It can be quite a successful way of losing weight, but the weight immediately comes back on when the diet is terminated. The diet raises the good cholesterol, but it is not clear if the high consumption of fat will be good for anyone in the long run.

Doctors may be able to restore a body damaged by an unfortunate accident or by an assault of a killer bug, but don't depend on them to maintain you in optimum health. That is your responsibility. There are several options available to each of us, all of which are entirely under our control. Be optimistic and positive in your outlook — it enhances the functioning of your immune system. Cultivate the right circle of friends. Avoid people who tempt you with unhealthy habits. If all your friends are couch potatoes you will become one yourself. If all your friends are exercising, stretching their minds and stretching their bodies, you are likely to do the same. Drink more water and eat less food. Supplement regular meals with vitamins, and other anti-oxidants, and do some active exercise that will make your pulse speed up. You will not only live longer, you will better enjoy what life has to offer.

Preventive Medicine is fashionable today and rightly so. Alternative Medicine, herbal medicine, Chinese medicine, and other homeopathic alternatives may all have merits too, but watch out for the hype. Ask yourself if the promoters of certain health products are really interested in your well-being, or more interested in padding their own pockets.

Exercise the brain with simple mental challenges on a regular basis especially when you pass the age of seventy. Try to memorize telephone numbers, subtract sevens starting at a hundred, recite a poem, or memorize a new one. You may delay or perhaps even avert the onset of Alzheimer's disease.

Take a baby Aspirin every day. The adult Aspirin, coated or not, can promote bruising, even bleeding. A baby Aspirin, which is one quarter the dosage of the regular pill might be as effective in reducing the risk of strokes, heart attacks, and colon cancer, without the side effects of a regular tablet. Of course, if you have already had a stroke or a heart attack and if your doctor has you taking the 325 mg tablet daily, you must comply with this regimen. The risks of bruising and bleeding are still there, but these risks are worth taking in these circumstances.

Focus on an object far away, then on something near. Without moving your head, look in all four directions. In other words, exercise the muscles of your eyes. The connection of the eye muscles to the brain may, when exercised, stimulate better memory, according to recent reports. Stretch the muscles in your neck by rotating your head and moving it up and down as far as you can. Stretch your arm muscles by swinging them forwards and backward and then with arms horizontal, swing them back as far as you can, as you did under the direction of gym teachers years ago. Touch your toes without bending your knees. Stand on one foot, and pull up your other foot to touch your buttocks. Stretch every muscle you can. Once you get the process going, consult books and magazine articles on the subject. Remember, start the exercises first; then go to the books. Reading articles does not burn off sufficient calories, and detailed instructions are just going to turn you off. Floss your teeth. Correct bad breath, it's distasteful to everyone. Remember that as you age, your food requirements lessen. Maintain the same intake, and you will inevitably put on weight. This process kicks in when you reach age thirty-five. The advice to eat less food and drink more water makes sense.

Keep the bowels regular by paying attention to the food you eat. We may be what we eat. Prunes and bran are fine, but try to stay away from laxatives on a regular basis. The more laxatives you use, the more you will need. On the other hand, there is nothing wrong with stool softeners, like docusate.

Practice the Kegel exercise regularly. Stop the urine in mid-flow and contract the muscle you have used to do so on a regular basis, in between urination. Bad bladder habits are easily acquired and can be corrected by willing the bladder to behave better. The Kegel exercise is one example of establishing control of involuntary muscles, those normally under the control of the autonomic or involuntary nervous system. In like fashion, get more control of other automatic functions, like breathing, pulse, and blood pressure. Breathe in deeply, and exhale slowly. The monks in Zen training are taught to count their breathing and place their minds on the pits of their bellies. As you gain more body control, the pulse should slow and the blood pressure should fall.

There is no easy road. Stretch your mind and stretch your muscles. Don't be fooled by easy solutions, a pill, a magic potion, or a nonsense diet. Health, like a skill, is something you develop by dedicated practice.

Recently a book was written about the Okinawa life style. People living on this tiny island just off the main islands of Japan live longer than anybody else anywhere in the world. When the natives move off the island their lifespans return to the norm of their new culture. The reason for the longevity, then, must be in the diet, attitude, and life style in Okinawa. Just what did the investigators discover? The elderly Okinawa natives eat very little animal fat, and they have a high intake of complex carbohydrate and isoflavones in their diet. They believe in active exercise, and their national attitude is upbeat. Ninety year old men and women are actively working the farm. Shangri La, they remind us, is certainly within our grasp.

The biotechnology revolution has already begun, with potentially exciting outcomes for all of us. Like any new science, it is starting slowly; however, I expect that its momentum will pick up considerably in the next few years. What follows is my understanding of this new phenomenon.

Quantum physics gave birth to the computer and the laser. These made the human genome project, the mapping of the genetic blue-print of mankind, possible. Our destiny may be controlled by the genes, in large measure, but the environment may be responsible for the activation or inactivation of these tiny bits of the human blueprint. What we have here is comparable to the nature-nurture argument for intelligence. Genes may play a major role but the environment has no insignificant effect.

The mapping of the human genome can have enormous implications to health. What can it mean to cancer?

Genes that promote cancer are called *oncogenes*. Many have already been identified, and others will be discovered and named in the days to come. Watch out for these disclosures. I fully expect that we will find some disease-specific genes, located on their parent chromosomes, before the end of this decade. Sometimes, the presence of one particular oncogene may be sufficient for a particular cancer to develop. Often, though, cancer occurs not only with the presence of an oncogene, but with its interaction with what are called *tumor suppressor genes*. Many of these genes have been identified, the one most frequently mentioned being the one called P-53. This gene, located on the 17th chromosome, can be damaged at any one of over one hundred sites in its molecular structure, and its absence or damage can promote one of a multitude of cancers, including those with an origins in the lung, breast, prostate, bladder, kidney, pancreas, brain, and colon, among others. It seems likely that the tumor suppressor genes are affected by the environment, that is, by the food we eat or the air we breathe.

Once cancer develops, the malignant cells become immortal, the life-fuse that normally shortens with each division does not do so with cancer cells. This fuse is called a *telomere* and what keeps it from shortening is called *telomerase*, present in cancer cells, and absent in healthy cells. Every cell in our body is programmed to die after a finite number of divisions. This process of programmed cell death is called *apoptosis* and fails to occur with cancer cells.

The spread of cancer to other sites is encouraged when there is an absence of a kind of glue, called *E-cadherins*, and promoted by the development of new blood vessels in a process known as *angiogenesis*. Without angiogenesis, cancer cells remain dormant, according to Judah Folkman, the father of angiogenesis. When there is a defect in a naturally occurring angiogenesis inhibitor, like *endostatin*, malignancies, like prostate cancer, occur two or three times as often as a clinical problem. When endostatin occurs in abundance, as happens in Down's syndrome, solid cancers, such as those we see in the prostate, do not occur. I mention these technical terms only to point out that when chemical processes are understood, antagonist drugs are inevitable consequences.

Experimental gene therapy and experimental immuno-therapy, as they apply to cancer management, are in their infancies. The underlying principle behind these man-made manipulations is, nevertheless, sound. Consider the following:

As viruses, unlike bacteria, can exist only within live cells, why not infect the cancer cells with a virus that has a limited life span. When the virus dies, the cell harboring the virus, presumably the cancer cell, dies. Alternatively, infect the cancer cells with a virus for which we have an established killing agent. Let the virus thrive for a while then zap it with the lethal agent. These tricks are called experimental gene therapies. In one ingenious maneuver, the gene that codes for the glow of the firefly, called the *Luciferase* gene, is incorporated into the virus. If the cancer cell glows, it is visible proof that the virus must have invaded it.

In experimental immuno-therapy, killed cancer cells are exposed to cells that process them, so that they will be recognized as foreign, and thus stimulate an immune response. These processing cells, called *dendritic cells*, are harvested from just under the skin where they reside, or from the blood, in a process called plasmapheresis, and are grown in vats outside the body. There is enormous promise in this kind of approach to destroy cancer cells, but since the products produced for one patient may not work for another, the process is both expensive and time-consuming.

Watch out for what is called "targeted therapy". This is the approach that has yielded spectacular results in the treatment of chronic myelogenous leukemia and certain stomach cancers. One magic pill is called Gleevec, made by Novartis. Others, like Avastin, by Genentech, Iressa, by Astra-Zeneca, and Erbitex by ImClone will find their role. How do they work?

Cancer cells have many receptors on their surfaces. When a molecule, called a growth factor, binds to it, it is as though a switch has been turned on to start a car engine. There is a cascade of further reactions. Scientists have developed chemicals to block the different receptors. The epithelial growth factor, for example, is blocked by Iressa and Erbitex. Other products will be developed to interrupt the cascade of reactions that follow. What we know today is simply the beginning.

Cancer will be conquered with agents developed against *telomerase, E-cadherins, angiogenesis, or oncogenes*, and with the restoration or repair of the different *tumor suppressor genes*. It's only a question of time. Stay alive and profit from the biotechnology revolution.

Laugh and encourage the immune system, add anti-oxidants to stabilize the DNA, cut down animal fats and don't touch cigarettes unless you are suicidal. Become proactive about your health. Give yourself a fair and fighting chance.

Life has been described, rather accurately if you think about it, as a sexually transmitted terminal illness, but there is no need to speed up the process. As one of my patients put it: "Life is like a roll of toilet paper: the closer you get to the end, the faster it spins." It's bad enough that there are toxins in the air we breathe, but there are also killer bugs, that not only adapt to the drugs devised in the laboratories, but jump species from animals to human. AIDS and Ebola from apes, Creutzfeldt-Jakov (mad cow) from cattle, West Nile from birds, SARS from civet, and bird-like flu from poultry are among this deadly group. Changes in diet and lifestyles are within our control and are, therefore, choices we should exercise.

Actually, in the Zen world, there is no difference between life and death. To live is to be born every minute. The moment you cease being born, there is death. The cells in our body are dying and being born every moment. We do not die with the cells we were born with. Some of our cells live for just a few hours, some for days, and other for much longer, but our cells are always turning over. We choose to define death with the stop of the heart beat, but we do recognize that a person can be brain-dead long before the cessation of cardiac activity. People who have not contemplated their existence have never lived, according to the philosophers. "Do not make such a fuss about dying," Zen says, "because life and death are ongoing processes. Instead, make every moment as precious as the next."

Portrait by Eric Wesselow (1990)

Racial Discrimination

A long and fulfilling life can be the reward of healthy habits, as I have suggested. What about healthy race relations? Can that be cultivated as well?

I have no desire to return to my youth – as a whole, that was a painful period of my life. I am not alone believing that "youth is wasted on the young" as Bernard Shaw observed. Jonathan Swift said: "No wise man ever wishes to be younger," and Oscar Wilde said: "No man is rich enough to buy back his past." We do not get smarter as we get older but we do get wiser.

In Tokyo once, when I was with my son, we encountered a loud demonstration. We were asked to sign our names in support.

"What would we be supporting?" I asked.

"Fair treatment of the Koreans in Japan," I was told.

Traditionally, the native Japanese were racist. They felt superior to the Koreans, Chinese, and other orientals. They believed their intestinal tracts to be longer than those of other people, and that they processed food and drugs differently. They believed they were superior creations: "When God made man," they said, "He left his creation too long in the oven and produced the black man. Then He took his creation too soon out of the oven and made the white man, and when He had it just right, He made the Japanese." The Japanese have not endeared themselves to people in other lands with this kind of attitude.

Even with their defeat in World War II, their sense of superiority has remained intact. They justify a no-immigration policy on the grounds that their small islands cannot support newcomers. They are unfair to the Chinese, Koreans, and other orientals. Many Chinese and Korean natives in Japan change their names into Japanese so that they can better compete. They have discriminated openly against the Japanese who have lived abroad, labeling them "hiki-age-sha", a condescending term, and they have treated women as inferior beings. I remember a wife of a doctor telling me: "When we were in America, my husband opened doors for me, carried my bags, and walked beside me, but as soon as we returned to Japan, things changed. He got off the airplane at Narita with two suitcases, walked ahead, dropped them to the ground, and expected me to pick them up and follow him." Many female scientists have sought refuge in America certain they had no chances of advancement in their native land. Japan needs to clean up its act.

And America? Young countries in North and South America, populated by immigrants or descendants of immigrants, like Canada and the USA, are designated by socially acceptable labels. The USA is called a "melting pot" because the immigrants there are supposed to have relinquished their ties to their land of origin, intermarried, and become a nation of mixed races. Canada, on the other hand, is supposed to be populated by people who still cherish their ties to their lands of origin, and celebrate the cultural diversity, or the 'cultural mosaic' that constitutes the land.

Of course this sociological designation is flawed. It's only people of the white races who are invited into the melting pot in the U.S.A. while, in Canada, immigrants, like the Japanese, are intermarried to people outside their community more often than not. Recently released government data indicates that Canadians of Japanese ancestry are foremost in marrying outside their community.

As a Canadian from a visible minority community, I have faced taunts, insults, and outright discrimination. I have also been assigned status and credit I may not deserve, like the presumption of extra dexterity or extra intelligence because of my Japanese ancestry. What do I make of it? The experiences have taught me to be vigilant about making judgements about people. As the bible says: *Judge not that ye be not judged.* I can live with that. Do not take extra pride in a racial origin, nor assume extra shame. Racists and bigots should be publicly condemned at every turn, whether they be politicians in power, Nobel laureates, famous scientists, or men of letters. Rich and famous people are often racists, sometimes without even realizing it, comfortable with their prejudices because their beliefs have not interfered with their seeming success. One of my childhood heroes was Bob Feller, ace strike-out pitcher for the Cleveland Indians. What a disappointment it was for me to discover that Feller believed that the black man did not belong in professional baseball.

I have no qualms taking a strong stance against racism in any form. If you are not black, you cannot begin to appreciate what it means to be called a "nigger." If you are not oriental, you cannot appreciate the emotion evoked by the word "Chink" or "Jap." These choice words have more sting than any four-letter word or finger gestures.

It strikes me now that in my zeal to condemn racism in any form, I may have been unfairly critical of the people of my ancestry. Are the Japanese, in fact, more racist than other people? I don't think they are, but they had been brain-washed a generation ago by a kind of institu-tionalized racism, the kind that makes them out to be superior creations – God's special children. The Germans of the thirties and forties were fed the same pap by their leaders, to their eventual regret, as have countless citizenries, by their misguided governments. My contention is that any of this foolish racial or religious superiority is just that; foolishness. The task we face is to recognize it for what it is and to fight it at every opportunity.

I had a professor friend, a gentleman named Raymond Klibansky, who was a world-renowned, highly respected philosopher. At one time he was the professor of Philosophy, both of McGill stories of how the people at M16 coated their stomachs with sardine oil before attending cocktail parties so that they would not be guilty of the "loose lips that sink ships." Ian Fleming of James Bond fame and Bill Stevenson, who wrote "The Man Called Intrepid," among others, were his underlings and, rather second rate, according to him.

The late Professor Klibansky is associated today with one powerful word — toleration. He had been instrumental in freeing dissidents, in many countries, through organizations like Amnesty International. He represented what the world needs — more tolerance.

Judging a person by his creed, color, or ethnic origin is abhorrent to most people. But, being anti-racist is not necessarily being pro multi-cultural. The line may be blurred but there is a subtle difference. I think it is appropriate to have pride in your ethnicity but it should be secondary to your love and patriotism to the country that has adopted you as its citizen. I do not believe turbans belong in the dress code of the Royal Canadian Mounted Police any more than do kilts or kimonos. I do not favor tax dollars supporting most multi-cultural endeavors. I think affirmative action demeans the accomplishments of people from the visible minorities. I think countries which take in immigrants can and should impose conditions on their new citizens. Loyalties cannot exist to different countries on an equal basis. Equal treatment under the law should be sufficient for any group.

The problem, in young countries like Canada and the USA, is not an inferiority complex of the visible minorities, as much as it is the superiority complex of the dominant majority. This complex may be at a subconscious level, more covert than overt. Why, for example, do many Canadians of French origin in Quebec clamor for extra recognition as descendants of one of the founding nations? Why should a family going back seven generations have more claim to a country than a family that goes back two generations? By that argument extra special status must be accorded the native population. And look at what special considerations, like freedom from taxes on cigarettes and alcohol, have done to our aboriginal population. The special status has been a form of genocide.

There is, I think, a certain arrogance among descendants of the Anglo-Saxons. It's subtle, it's in the body language; it's there when he says: "What do you expect? He's from the Caribbean, or he's a black, a Chink, or a Jap." The quintessential American Anglo-Saxon, H. L. Mencken, has said of his compatriots: "What are the characters that I discern most clearly in the Anglo-Saxon type of man? I may answer at once that two stick out above all others. One is his curious and apparently incurable incompetence — his congenital inability to do any difficult thing easily and well, whether it be isolating a bacillus or writing a sonata. The other is his astounding susceptibility to fears and alarms — in short, his hereditary cowardice." Now, if a black man said that of the blacks, he would be loudly condemned; if an oriental man said that of the orientals, he would be publicly chastised. But, when an Anglo-Saxon says that of the whites, we are amused and wonder if it was said tongue-in-cheek.

As long as members of the visible minorities are subjected to taunts "How come you speak English so good?" there will be requests for the recognition of ethnicity. It's only natural. My plea is not that we end racial prejudice; that is unlikely, but rather to diminish it deliberately, until, one day, it may dissipate, even disappear.

The call to take a deliberate stance against racism is reinforced by events in my own life. Some years ago my son was held up at gunpoint by a large black man who demanded he pass over his money and his watch. My son had little cash in his possession and felt the sum was unlikely to satisfy the gunman.

"Why don't we walk down to the automatic bank machine and I will withdraw what I have," my son said, fully cognizant that his balance was minimal. He withdrew what he had, passed it over, and tried to engage him in conversation. The man with the gun ordered him to walk on without looking back. "I thought he might turn trigger-happy and shoot me for the fun of it," my son said. After this episode, my son said every big black man gave him the shivers. I have to admit I had to make a conscious and deliberate effort to convince myself that the gunman could have been white, yellow or brown. It is incidents such as this one, which convince me of the great challenges we face when we are personally involved in an incident which, although it has no race attached to it, can, nevertheless, lead to profiling. As a member of a racial minority, I am more than sensitive to this fact and I must admit, in all candor, that I do not have a ready solution to this problem.

And, certainly, the events of September 11, 2001 reinforce the thought. Just because the terrorists were all of middle eastern background it does not mean that all middle eastern men are terrorists. Sometimes, the prejudices we harbor are hard to lay aside, especially when loved ones have been the victims of terror, however, if we are to survive as a species, we must.

President Bush's war on terrorism has received uneven but undeniably widespread support in the USA. The Bush response to terrorism, though, is not Christian. The Christian response to Sept 11 should have been to share the American wealth with the have-not countries. It should drop gifts, not bombs. Consider the possible rhetoric from the other side: "We know of an evil empire. It has dropped nuclear bombs on civilian cities that have wiped out more than 200,000 lives. It will not tolerate the development of nuclear arsenal in other countries but it will not destroy its own stockpile. This evil empire is the USA." Can we say that these charges are wrong? As former USA president Jimmy Carter wisely proclaimed: "War may sometimes be a necessary evil. But, no matter how necessary, it is always evil."

Recently, I attended the fiftieth reunion of our high school class. I was struck with how little we have changed in our basic gestures and mannerisms despite the passage of years. The tilt of the head, the hand gestures, the manner of speech, the swagger, the resignation, the twinkle, or the look of utter disgust I associated with a particular classmate was still there, fifty years later, despite physical changes, like receding hairlines, stoop, or paunch. So much of what we are is due to the genes. Furthermore, the fact that I could remember these attributes of my class-mates, but not much else, reinforced in my mind how much of what we remember is emotional and not intellectual.

And, I have now observed two generations of doctors-in-training, a total number that approaches or may even exceed one hundred, including one father and son combination. If surgical training was so meaningful the residents should acquire the mannerisms of the teachers; instead, I saw the father and the son handle tissue and surgical instruments in exactly the same way. If we are to advance as a species we must deliberately change our behavior, genetic make-up alone will not ensure that.

Summing Up

Here is the five minute speech on Zen and Surgery I delivered in the Spring of 2001.

Ms. Chairman, Ladies and Gentlemen:

I want to take this opportunity to say something about teaching surgical skills to the (Urology) residents-in-training. I have never spoken about this in a public forum before, and I do so now with some trepidation, because it is a very personal story. I am going to talk about a connection that exists, I believe, between Zen and the practice of surgery.

My father was a young man when he came to Canada and was converted to Christianity. He was very devout and being a Christian was what best defined him. I was raised in the faith and I am grateful for the many valuable precepts Christianity has taught me — Love thy neighbor. Turn the other cheek. God is Love.

But, in middle age I got curious about Buddhism, Zen Buddhism in particular. I read widely: books by Daisetz T Suzuki, Philip Kapleau, Alan Watts, Christmas Humphreys, among many others and, it came as a shocking revelation for me to discover that Zen Buddhism was not a religion at all. It didn't qualify because Zen does not contemplate the Almighty, nor the Hereafter. Zen Buddhism is, simply, a philosophy. Thus, it is perfectly reasonable for a Christian to be a Zen devotee. It is not necessary to renounce one for the other. The two are not incompatible.

Furthermore, I discovered that when I am doing good surgery, and I have to tell you, I do a lot of that, I am in a state of Zen. We are all often in this state. You are in a state of Zen when you are comfortably on your bicycle going from point A to point B. You are not riding in a state of Zen when you are learning: when you have to worry about keeping the bicycle upright, and struggling to coordinate the foot on the pedal and the hands on the handle bar at the same time. It was Zen when Babe Ruth pointed to the field and hit the ball out of the park: his mind was not on whether he would hit or miss, his mind was on putting the ball out there. Let me remind you about the story of the centipede. It was merrily walking along on its two hundred feet when it was asked: How do you remember which foot to place before the other? (I paused, for effect.) *It could no longer walk!* (A warm ripple percolated through the room, and I knew I had the rapt attention of the audience.)

A Zen surgeon does his job free of preoccupation, without agitation, smoothly, calmly effortlessly. How do I achieve that in the training resident? There are four points to be made. Firstly, I do this by being a role model, by projecting a cool calmness that is real, not feigned, and not artificial.

Secondly, I do this by insisting upon repetitive, ad nauseum, practicing of routine maneuvers, like tying surgical knots, or handling surgical instruments until those maneuvers can be done smoothly and swiftly.

Thirdly, I do this by reducing complex procedures into a series of objectives that the resident must be able to recite to me, forward and backward.

Fourthly, I do this by encouraging, by praising, by cheering, by reinforcing the positives. In teaching surgical skills, the carrot works a lot better than the stick. You don't produce a good surgeon by criticizing, reprimanding, humiliating, and belittling.

It must be working because the residents voted me the best teacher in Urology last year, and this year, the university is honoring me with this award. It is very gratifying to me and I shall cherish this award as one of the best recognition I have ever received. I thank you very much.

Dr. Steinert thanked me warmly and said she wondered how I was going to make the link between Zen and surgical training — until I had done it! A number of young students sought me out to tell me how much they appreciated what I had to say. A doctor, with an East Indian background said she was going to pay more attention to her roots. My own colleagues did not exactly shower me with praise but neither did they treat me like a heretic. My students were the most generous in their assessment. One resident said he was going to pursue medical education as a career and that he would accentuate the positives as I had suggested.

Inadvertently and unintentionally, I have stumbled upon the six big secrets of life. I have alluded to them in the text, but it is time to enumerate them. Here they are:

1. Be charitable – that is the core of Christianity.
2. Be compassionate regardless of consequences, and do whatever you do, be it a physical act or a mental challenge, with a mind freed of preoccupation – that is the essence of Zen.
3. Make learning an emotional event – bring passion into the process.
4. Enjoy your work so that it will not feel like work.
5. Actively promote your own health.
6. Be tolerant of others and beware of prejudices.

Not a bad nor difficult set of rules to live by. When I suggested to friends that I was attempting to write a book on the "Six Secrets of Life" almost everybody I spoke to thought I was referring to "Sex Secrets." I admit the term "secrets" can have odious connotations. It conjures up images of secret societies, cults, and even of the occult. It may have been more accurate to ruminate about the "six principles" or the "six precepts of life," but "secrets" has a better ring to it.

The admonition to disengage the mind (to perform well), but to engage the emotion (to learn) may seem contradictory, but I don't think it is. Does it not make sense to practice long and hard, and then to perform any task with a mind freed of all preoccupations? And, does it not make sense to bring passion to the learning process? Reducing Christianity and Zen Buddhism to a single sentence may seem unfair, but we have gotten into trouble over the years because of the man-made over interpretations of religious precepts. Christians search the bible to find arguments for or against homosexuality, for example, instead of dwelling on "Love thy neighbor." Buddhists overly emphasize a respect for all living creatures over compassion for our fellow man.

Christianity's Holy Trinity escapes me still but, lo and behold, the meaning of the Three Treasures of Buddhism has become clear. Buddha, the peaceful perfection, says that performance must always occur with a stilled mind; Dharma, the true teaching says "rid yourself of interfering thoughts"; and Sangha, the true brotherhood, says enlightenment will occur, when one behaves compassionately at all times, with no regard for reward or recognition.

Let me end my account with a short anecdote. A Zen monk opens a hot-dog stand. A customer makes a purchase and hands over a twenty dollar bill. After a while, a good while, he asks:

"Where's my change?"

"Change," the monk replies, " must come from within."

Does the joke offend? I think not. I can imagine my Zen-master friend, Dr. Hori, roaring with laughter.

PRINTED IN THE YEAR
TWO THOUSAND
SIX
BY
GUÉRIN, PUBLISHERS
MONTREAL, QUEBEC.